Investigating Natural Disasters
Through Children's Literature

Investigating Natural Disasters Through Children's Literature

An Integrated Approach

Anthony D. Fredericks

2001
Teacher Ideas Press
A Division of
Libraries Unlimited, Inc.
Englewood, Colorado

TEACHER IDEAS PRESS
A Division of
Libraries Unlimited, Inc.
P.O. Box 6633
Englewood, CO 80155-6633
1-800-237-6124
www.lu.com/tip

Library of Congress Cataloging-in-Publication Data

Fredericks, Anthony D.
    Investigating natural disasters through children's literature : an integrated approach / Anthony D. Fredericks.
        p. cm.
    Includes bibliographical references (p.   ).
    ISBN 1-56308-861-4 (pbk.)
    1. Natural disasters--Study and teaching (Elementary) 2. Natural disasters--Juvenile literature. 3. Best books. I. Title.

GB5005 .F74 2001
372.83--dc21
                                                                00-051154

Contents

When I was young, natural disasters fascinated me. I grew up in southern California—in Los Angeles and Newport Beach. In elementary school, we would practice the requisite "earthquake drill" twice a year. We were taught how to crawl under our desks, curl up in a semi-fetal position, put our hands over our heads, and close our eyes. Our teachers told us that we lived in an earthquake-prone area, and it was necessary for us to know what to do in case one should strike during school hours.

I also remember at least two instances when small earthquakes struck southern California. As I recall, each one came in the middle of the night and shook the house—not violently but hard enough so that my sisters and I felt the overwhelming need to race to our parents' bedroom and crawl under the covers for the remainder of the night. Although I didn't understand the science behind those tremors, I certainly did gain a respect for their power and the rationale behind those twice-a-year earthquake drills at school.

Even as an adult, I am still mesmerized by the power and intensity of natural disasters— particularly how they influence and effect the lives of so many people around the world. I have watched a bone-jarring avalanche thunder down a mountainside, seen the incendiary and explosive power of an erupting volcano up close, witnessed the devastation of a hurricane days after it swept through southern Florida, talked with one of the world's leading experts on tsunamis, and listened to my own son (who lives in Colorado) tell me about the time he was struck by lightning one summer day while hiking through the mountains. (If you are interested in reading a spine-tingling and heart-stopping account of this specific event, log on to http://www.cmc.org/cmc/rpt/democrat.html.) As a result, I have grown to appreciate these events, not just for their enormous power (did you know that there's enough energy in 10 minutes of one hurricane to match the nuclear stockpiles of the world?), but also for their incredible frequency (did you know that 100 bolts of lightning strike the surface of Earth every second?).

As a children's author, I frequently have the pleasure of traveling to schools around the country to share my books and my experiences as a writer. Because most of my children's books focus on nonfiction accounts of nature, Earth science, and the environment, I am often inundated with questions about various types of natural phenomena: "How hot does lava get?" "What was the highest tsunami in the world?" "Have you ever been in a tornado?" "Have *you* ever been hit by lightning?" It is quite evident that not only do most youngsters have an abiding interest in natural disasters, they also have a keen desire to learn more about these events. This interest becomes particularly evident when the media reports a hurricane threatening the East Coast of the United States, a volcano violently erupting in northern Japan, a series of funnel clouds dancing along a stretch of "Tornado Alley," or an unexpected tsunami that has wiped out a dozen villages in a chain of Pacific Ocean islands.

Investigating Natural Disasters Through Children's Literature emanated from my own experiences with natural phenomena, the fascinating research I've conducted for my children's books, and my work as a classroom teacher in helping students develop an appreciation for the role of science in their lives. This book also grew out of conversations with fellow teachers around the country who were looking for innovative ways to help students appreciate natural disasters and their influence in our lives.

It is my hope that you will discover within these pages an infinite variety of creative learning possibilities for your classroom and that your students will discover an exciting diversity of mind-expanding, concept-building, and real-world experiences, experiences that will help them develop a respect and admiration for the power of nature *and* the power of scientific investigation.

—Tony Fredericks

Part 1

Children's Literature and Natural Disasters

Chapter 1

Introduction

May 3, 1999

Carrie Anderson, frightened and sobbing, wrapped herself in her mother's arms under a highway overpass just outside Oklahoma City. Their car lay abandoned on the roadway as the two of them huddled against the concrete pillars that would be their only hope for survival. Less than half a mile away, an F-5 tornado with wind speeds of up to 318 miles per hour raked the countryside, devastating everything in its path. Houses imploded, cars were tossed like dish rags, telephone poles became deadly sabers, and lives—thousands of lives—hung in the balance as the Chichasha twister (as it was to be named) ripped an 80-mile gash over the cities and suburbs of central Oklahoma. For nearly 20 hours, mid-America was overwhelmed and overrun by the sound and fury of nature's wrath.

Carrie and her mother survived, but the scene of destruction left behind was both awesome and sobering: 45 people lost their lives, and more than 750 individuals were injured. Property damage exceeded $1 billion. Homes, businesses, and entire neighborhoods were literally blown away—unrecognizable even to those who had lived there all their lives. It was the worst tornado in U.S. history—a natural disaster full of fury, devastation, and tragedy. It would be forever etched on the minds of Carrie Anderson and her family, as it would be on the thousands of Oklahomans who endured it and the millions of people all across the country who watched it on the evening news.

The Science of Natural Disasters

Natural disasters have always been with us. They are part of the mystery and majesty of nature. They are part of our history and heritage. They are as inevitable as the sunrise, yet as unpredictable as the weekly lottery. We have studied them, experienced them, tracked them, and lived through them. We have come away amazed and awe-struck by their beauty and their might. They are a testament to the dynamic nature of the Earth—an evolving, changing, transforming body that is never static, never passive. History has been altered by natural disasters, and natural disasters have created history. They are our past, our present, and will certainly be part of our future.

Students, too, have always been fascinated with natural disasters. It may be because they are larger than life, because they are so powerful, or because they are so awesome. Suffice it to say that volcanoes, hurricanes, earthquakes, and tsunamis have enthralled generations of youngsters with their potency, devastation, and might. So, too, are natural disasters phenomena that offer students opportunities to study and understand some of the forces of nature: the ever-changing Earth, the dynamics of weather patterns, the ceaseless energy of water, the majesty of the ocean, and the rage of fire.

This book is designed to offer you and your students a participatory approach to the study of natural disasters, an approach asserting that when educators complement the study of science (particularly the science of natural disasters) with engaging and relevant children's literature, children will have a plethora of opportunities to comprehend these forces and examine them far beyond the rudimentary knowledge provided in their science textbooks. The emphasis in this book is on the processes of science—"hands-on, minds-on" activities, projects, exercises, and ventures that promote a personal response to science education and learning. Children's literature offers an array of investigative journeys and conceptual understandings that open students' eyes to the wonder of the world around them. Not only will students learn about the potency of nature, but they will be inspired to examine and explore the implications of that potency on the lives of people near and far.

The Literature-Based Approach to Natural Disasters

Many science programs are designed to give children a large quantity of information, have them memorize that data, and then ask them to recall the information on various assessment instruments. This may be a significant reason for students' less-than-enthusiastic response to science. That type of instruction does not allow for the active involvement of students in their own learning, nor does it allow children opportunities to think creatively about what they are learning.

My own experiences as a teacher has taught me that when students, no matter what their abilities or interests, are provided with opportunities to manipulate information in productive ways, learning becomes much more meaningful. I refer to this as a process approach to learning, an approach that provides students with an abundance of projects, activities, and instructional designs and allows them to make decisions and solve problems. In so doing, students get a sense that learning is much more than the commission of facts to memory. Rather, it is what children do with that knowledge that determines its impact on their attitudes and aptitudes.

A process approach to science is one in which children do something with the concepts and generalizations they learn. It implies that students can manipulate, decide, solve, predict, and structure the knowledge of science in ways that are meaningful to them. When teachers provide opportunities for students to actively process information, learning becomes more child centered and less text based. This results in a science program that is expansive, integrated, and dynamic.

A literature-based approach to science is a combination of activities, children's literature, "hands-on, minds-on" projects, and materials used to expand a science concept or idea. Literature-based science teaching and learning is multidisciplinary and multidimensional; it has no boundaries and no limits. In essence, a literature-based approach to science offers students a realistic arena within which they can learn and investigate science concepts for extended periods of time. It is a process approach to learning of the highest magnitude.

This approach to science instruction is built on the idea that learning can be integrative and multifaceted. A literature-based approach to science education provides children with a host of opportunities to become actively involved in the dynamics of their own learning. In so doing, they will be able to draw positive relationships between what "happens" in the classroom and what is happening outside the classroom. Literature-based teaching promotes science education as a sustaining and relevant venture.

Science Teaching and Multiple Intelligences

Literature-based instruction in science offers a host of opportunities for students to actively engage in a constructivist approach to learning. It offers a variety of meaningful learning opportunities tailored to students' needs and interests. Children are given the chance to make important choices about what they learn, as well as about how they learn it. Literature-based instruction provides the means to integrate the science program with the rest of the elementary curriculum while involving students in a multiplicity of learning opportunities and ventures.

Incorporated into literature-based explorations are opportunities for students to take advantage of, hone, and build upon one or more of their multiple intelligences. According to Howard Gardner (*Frames of Mind: The Theory of Multiple Intelligences.* New York: Basic Books, HarperCollins Publishers, 1985), each individual possesses eight different intelligences (see Table 1.1) in varying degrees. These intelligences (as opposed to a single intelligence quotient as traditionally reported via many standardized intelligence tests) help determine how individuals learn and how they fare in their daily lives. Gardner defined an "intelligence" as consisting of three components:

1.   The ability to create an effective product or offer a service that is valuable in one's culture

2.   A set of skills that enables an individual to solve problems encountered in life

3.   The potential for finding or creating solutions for problems, which enables a person to acquire new knowledge

Individuals differ in the strength (or weakness) of each of the eight intelligences in isolation as well as in combination. For example, whereas some individuals learn best through linguistic means, others are more kinesthetic learners, and still others are spatial learners. Suffice to say that no two people learn in the same way, nor should they be taught in the same way.

Table 1.1.
The Eight Human Intelligences

According to Howard Gardner, individuals possess these eight intelligences in varying degrees.

1. Verbal-Linguistic Intelligence involves ease in producing language and sensitivity to the nuances, order, and rhythm of words. Individuals who are strong in verbal-linguistic intelligence love to read, write, and tell stories. Enhancement activities: writing, reading, storytelling, speaking, debating.

2. Logical-Mathematical Intelligence relates to the ability to reason deductively or inductively and to recognize and manipulate abstract patterns and relationships. Individuals who excel in this intelligence have strong problem-solving and reasoning skills and ask questions in a logical manner. Enhancement activities: problem solving, outlining, calculating, patterning, showing relationships.

3. Musical-Rhythmic Intelligence encompasses sensitivity to the pitch, timbre, and rhythm of sounds, as well as responsiveness to the emotional implications of these elements of music. Individuals who remember melodies or recognize pitch and rhythm exhibit musical intelligence. Enhancement activities: composing, singing, humming, making instrumental sounds, creating vibrations.

4. Visual-Spatial Intelligence includes the ability to create visual-spatial representations of the world and to transfer them mentally or concretely. Individuals who exhibit spatial intelligence need a mental or physical picture to best understand new information. They are strong in drawing, designing, and creating things. Enhancement activities: painting, drawing, sculpting, pretending, imagining.

5. Bodily-Kinesthetic Intelligence involves using the body to solve problems, make things, and convey ideas and emotions. Individuals who are strong in this intelligence are good at physical activities, eye-hand coordination, and have a tendency to move around, touch things, and gesture. Enhancement activities: dancing, miming, role playing, exercising, playing games.

6. Intrapersonal Intelligence entails the ability to understand one's own emotions, goals, and intentions. Individuals strong in intrapersonal intelligence have a strong sense of self, are confident, and can enjoy working alone. Enhancement activities: thinking strategies, focusing, metacognitive techniques, silent reflection, emotional processing.

7. Interpersonal Intelligence refers to the ability to work effectively with other people and to understand them and recognize their goals and intentions. Individuals who exhibit this intelligence thrive on cooperative work, have strong leadership skills, and are skilled at organizing, communicating, and negotiating. Enhancement activities: communicating, receiving feedback, collaborating, cooperating, structured feedback.

8. Naturalist Intelligence includes the capacity to recognize flora and fauna, to make distinctions in the natural world, and to use this ability productively in activities such as farming and biological science. Enhancement activities: planting, raising and tending, nurturing, observing, experimenting.

From Howard Gardner, *Frames of Mind: The Theory of Multiple Intelligences*
(New York: Basic Books, 1985).

The research on multiple intelligences has revealed that teaching aimed at sharpening one kind of intelligence will carry over to others. There is also mounting evidence that learning opportunities involving a variety of intelligences allow students to take advantage of their preferred intelligence(s), as well as to strengthen weaker intelligences. In short, literature-based instruction provides something for everyone.

Literature-based instruction allows teachers to extend, expand, and take advantage of students' intelligences. Literature-based instruction also provides many opportunities to combine the intelligences of students with the resources, information, and scientific principles of an entire science curriculum. In short, literature-based teaching celebrates multiple intelligences, offering learning opportunities that provide students with a meaningful and balanced approach to science learning. Above all, literature-based instruction supports and emphasizes the varied relationships that exist among science inquiry, a process approach to learning, and the exercise of multiple intelligences in a positive and supportive environment.

Advantages of Literature-Based Instruction

Literature-based instruction in science offers a plethora of advantages for both teachers and students. Table 1.2 synthesizes some of those benefits.

Table 1.2.
Advantages of Literature-Based Science Teaching

- Emphasizes and celebrates an individual's multiple intelligences in a supportive and creative learning environment.

- Focuses on the processes of science rather than the products of science.

- Reduces or eliminates the artificial barriers that often exist between curricular areas and provides an integrative approach to learning.

- Promotes a child-centered science curriculum, one in which students are encouraged to make their own decisions and to assume a measure of responsibility for learning.

- Stimulates self-directed discovery and investigation both in and out of the classroom.

- Assists youngsters in developing relationships between science ideas and concepts, thus enhancing appreciation and comprehension.

- Stimulates the creation of important science concepts through first-hand experiences and self-initiated discoveries.

- More time is available for instructional purposes. Science instruction does not have to be crammed into limited, artificial time periods but can be extended across the curriculum and throughout the day.

- The connections that can and do exist between science and other subjects, topics, and themes can be logically and naturally developed. Teachers can demonstrate relationships and assist students in comprehending those relationships.

(Continued)

Table 1.2. Advantages of Literature-Based Science Teaching (*continued*)

- Science can be promoted as a continuous activity, one not restricted by textbook designs, time barriers, or even the four walls of the classroom. Teachers can help students extend science learning into many aspects of their personal lives.

- Teachers are free to help students look at a science problem, situation, or topic from a variety of viewpoints, rather than the "right way" frequently demonstrated in a teacher's manual or curriculum guide.

- There is more emphasis on teaching students and less emphasis on telling students.

- Teachers can promote problem solving, creative thinking, and critical thinking processes within all dimensions of a topic.

Traditional approaches to science instruction rely primarily on packaged materials, usually in the form of commercial science series and the ubiquitous teacher's manual and student textbooks. A major disadvantage is that students often have the perception that science is textbook-based or that it takes place only during a specified time period of the school day. Literature-based instruction in science, however, provides students (and teachers) with an expanded curriculum, one without limits or boundaries. Table 1.3 compares some of the differences between literature-based instruction in science and more traditional forms of classroom organization such as textbooks and school or district curriculum guides.

Table 1.3.
Comparison of Literature-Based and Text-Based Curricula

Literature-Based Instruction	Textbook-Based Learning
Gives students a sense of ownership of their learning	Teacher makes all decisions about what will be learned and when
Facilitates responsible learning	Students are told what to do, but not always why
Is holistic in nature	Is fragmented and disconnected
Encourages risk taking	Emphasizes the accumulation of "right" answers
Promotes inquiry and reflection	Teacher asks most of the questions and has most of the answers
Breaks down artificial curricular boundaries; integrates the entire curriculum	Segmented and divided curriculum is imposed
Encourages collaborative and cooperative learning	Students attempt to get high marks or good grades (vis-à-vis tests and exams)

Literature-Based Instruction	Textbook-Based Learning
Teacher models appropriate learning behaviors	Teacher dictates learning behaviors
Assessment is authentic, meaningful, and infused throughout the learning process	Assessment occurs at the end of learning a predetermined body of knowledge and is teacher-controlled
Encourages self-direction and individual inquiries	Everyone must learn the same body of knowledge
Students understand the why of what they're learning	Students are told what to learn
Allows students to make approximations of learning	Students must learn absolutes
Promotes, supports, and stimulates multiple intelligences	Everyone learns through a formal, standardized lecture and recitation process

Literature-based instruction facilitates the teaching of science as much as the learning of science. The entire science curriculum is broadened, strengthened, and made more attentive to the development of individual science competencies.

Chapter 2

Making Connections

The inclusion of children's literature within the science curriculum should be a natural and normal part of students' experiences with science. It provides youngsters with valuable opportunities to extend and expand their knowledge of the world and to develop a rich appreciation for the science concepts, values, and generalizations contained within good literature. By infusing books and literature into science programs, teachers help their students understand that science is much more than a dry accumulation of facts and figures. They help students explore and investigate the immediate and far-flung world in an arena that knows no limits.

The use of literature within science is based on several precepts:

1. Literature provides an ever-expanding array of information in a welcome and familiar format to students.

2. Literature extends the science curriculum beyond textbook constraints.

3. Literature relates to children's lives in diverse and divergent ways.

4. Literature, both fiction and nonfiction, helps children understand their scientific heritage.

5. Literature assists children in developing positive attitudes toward themselves and the world in which they live.

6. Literature provides vicarious *and* firsthand experiences with all science concepts.

7. Literature provides students with new information and knowledge unobtainable in any other format.

8. Literature stimulates creative thinking and problem-solving abilities in a variety of contexts.

9. Literature opens up the world and draws students in to make self-initiated discoveries.

10. Literature is fun!

When quality literature is a significant part of the science program, children can become involved in activities and gain experiences to which they may not be exposed within a text-based program.

National Science Education Standards

In response to a growing concern about the state of science education in the United States, hundreds of people (including teachers, school administrators, parents, curriculum coordinators, college faculty, scientists, engineers, and government officials) cooperated to develop an outline. This included a comprehensive list of what students need to know, understand, and be capable of doing to be scientifically literate.

The standards that resulted from this intensive examination of science education focus on a blending of "science as process" and "science as inquiry." This "hands-on, minds-on" approach to science education helps students actively develop their understanding of science by combining scientific knowledge with reasoning and thinking skills.

> The standards are based on the premise that science is an active process and that learning science is something that students do, not something that is done to them.

Not only do the standards provide an outline (as opposed to a curriculum) for the development of science instruction, they also bring coordination, consistency, and coherence to the improvement of science education. As such, they are organized into six broad categories: standards for science teaching, standards for professional development for teachers of science, standards for assessment in science, standards for science content, standards for science education programs, and standards for science education systems. Because effective teaching and coordinated content is at the heart of successful science education, this chapter will focus on the science teaching standards and the science content standards. The teaching and content standards are outlined in the tables below.

Table 2.1.

Teaching Standards

Teaching Standard A

Teachers of science plan an inquiry-based science program for their students. In doing this, teachers:

• Develop a framework of yearlong and short-term goals for students.

- Select science content and adapt and design curricula to meet the interests, knowledge, understanding, abilities, and experiences of students.

- Select teaching and assessment strategies that support the development of student understanding and nurture a community of science learners.

- Work together as colleagues within and across disciplines and grade levels.

Teaching Standard B

Teachers of science guide and facilitate learning. In doing this, teachers:

- Focus and support inquiries while interacting with students.

- Orchestrate discourse among students about scientific ideas.

- Challenge students to accept and share responsibility for their own learning.

- Recognize and respond to student diversity and encourage all students to participate fully in science learning.

- Encourage and model the skills of scientific inquiry, as well as the curiosity, openness to new ideas and data, and skepticism that characterize science.

Teaching Standard C

Teachers of science engage in ongoing assessment of their teaching and of student learning. In doing this, teachers:

- Use multiple methods and systematically gather data about student understanding and ability.

- Analyze assessment data to guide teaching.

- Guide students in self-assessment.

- Use student data, observations of teaching, and interactions with colleagues to reflect on and improve teaching practice.

- Use student data, observations of teaching, and interactions with colleagues to report student achievement and opportunities to learn to students, teachers, policy makers, and the general public.

Teaching Standard D

Teachers of science design and manage learning environments that provide students with the time, space, and resources needed for learning science. In doing this, teachers:

- Structure the time available so that students are able to engage in extended investigations.

- Create a setting for student work that is flexible and supportive of science inquiry.

- Ensure a safe working environment.

- Make the available science tools, materials, media, and technological resources accessible to students.

- Identify and use resources outside the school.

- Engage students in designing the learning environment.

(Continued)

Table 2.1. Teaching Standards (*continued*)

Teaching Standard E

Teachers of science develop communities of science learners that reflect the intellectual rigor of scientific inquiry and the attitudes and social values conducive to science learning. In doing this, teachers:

- Display and demand respect for the diverse ideas, skills, and experiences of all students.

- Enable students to have a significant voice in decisions about the content and context of their work and require students to take responsibility for the learning of all members of the community.

- Nurture collaboration among students.

- Structure and facilitate ongoing formal and informal discussions based on a shared understanding of rules of scientific discourse.

- Model and emphasize the skills, attitudes, and values of scientific inquiry.

Teaching Standard F

Teachers of science actively participate in the ongoing planning and development of the school science program. In doing this, teachers:

- Plan and develop the school science program.

- Participate in decisions concerning the allocation of time and other resources to the science program.

- Participate fully in planning and implementing professional growth and development strategies for themselves and their colleagues.

From the National Academy of Sciences, *National Science Education Standards* (Washington, D.C.: National Academy of Sciences, 1996), 30–52, 121–71.

Table 2.2.

Content Standards

Content Standard A (Science As Inquiry)

All students should develop:

Abilities necessary to do scientific inquiry (K–4, 5–8)
Understanding about scientific inquiry (K–4, 5–8)

Content Standard B (Physical Science)

All students should develop an understanding of

Properties of objects and materials (K–4)
Position and motion of objects (K–4)
Light, heat, electricity, and magnetism (K–4)
Properties and changes of properties in matter (5–8)
Motions and forces (5–8)
Transfer of energy (5–8)

Content Standard C (Life Science)

All students should develop an understanding of

> The characteristics of organisms (K–4)
> Life cycles of organisms (K–4)
> Organisms and environments (K–4)
> Structure and function in living systems (5–8)
> Reproduction and heredity (5–8)
> Regulation and behavior (5–8)
> Populations and ecosystems (5–8)
> Diversity and adaptations of organisms (5–8)

Content Standard D (Earth and Space Science)

All students should develop an understanding of

> Properties of Earth materials (K–4)
> Objects in the sky (K–4)
> Changes in Earth and sky (K–4)
> Structure of the Earth system (5–8)
> Earth's history (5–8)
> Earth in the solar system (5–8)

Content Standard E (Science and Technology)

All students should develop

> Abilities of technological design (K–4, 5–8)
> Understanding about science and technology (K–4, 5–8)
> Abilities to distinguish between natural objects and objects made by humans (K–4)

Content Standard F (Science in Personal and Social Perspectives)

All students should develop an understanding of

> Personal health (K–4, 5–8)
> Characteristics and changes in population (K–4)
> Types of resources (K–4)
> Changes in environments (K–4)
> Science and technology in local challenges (K–4)
> Populations, resources, and environments (5–8)
> Natural hazards (5–8)
> Risks and benefits (5–8)
> Science and technology in society (5–8)

Content Standard G (History and Nature of Science)

All students should develop an understanding of

> Science as a human endeavor (K–4, 5–8)
> Nature of science (5–8)
> History of science (5–8)

From the National Academy of Sciences, *National Science Education Standards* (Washington, D.C.: National Academy of Sciences, 1996), 30–52, 121–71.

In reviewing the standards above, it should be evident that many elements of those standards are embodied in the philosophy and design of a literature-based approach to science education. Equally important is the fact that those standards assist teachers in defining the structural components of effective lesson plans and units. In addition, they help define the environment in which that instruction can take place. The following description illustrates how one teacher integrated the teaching and content standards into a teaching plan.

A Sample Teaching Plan

Gail Fogerty has been teaching for almost 10 years in a school district just north of San Francisco. When she first began teaching fourth grade, her science program was "one broken microscope, some outdated textbooks, and lots of questions." Over the years, Gail has attended many science conferences, read dozens of teacher resource books ("My all-time favorite and the one I use most is *Science Adventures with Children's Literature: A Thematic Approach,*" Gail says), read scores of articles in *Science and Children*, and talked with fellow teachers in neighboring districts. As a result of her self-initiated research, Gail has become an ardent advocate of literature-based science instruction. In addition, she also believes that the National Science Education Standards have helped her create a learning environment in which she and her students can work together as active learners. Her science program is based on four assumptions: (1) a successful science curriculum is never static, (2) science instruction can be extended throughout the curriculum, (3) teachers should be facilitators rather than lecturers, and (4) student understanding of science is actively constructed through a wide variety of individual and social processes. Following is a single-day "lesson plan" that Gail used as part of a three-week unit titled The Changing Earth. Each of the activities, designs, and experiments is coded to one or more of the Science Teaching Standards, as well as to one or more of the Science Content Standards.

Theme: The Changing Earth

(Day 4: Volcanoes)

8:30–8:50 Opening

After putting away their book bags, students assemble around a table with several different daily newspapers (e.g., *San Francisco Chronicle, Los Angeles Times, New York Times*). Gail invites the students to look through the newspapers for articles regarding changes in the Earth (volcanic eruptions, earthquakes, landslides, etc.). They cut out selected articles and assemble them into an ongoing journal. One small group of students creates a dictionary booklet titled "My Earth Book." These pupils create a page for each letter of the alphabet (i.e., A = abyss, B = biosphere, C = chasm, D = dangerous). This group uses the book *Earth Words* by Seymour Simon (HarperCollins, 1995) as a reference for their dictionary. [Teaching Standards A, B, D, E; Content Standards A, F]

8:50–9:15 Whole Class Instruction

Gail shows the video *This Changing Planet* (National Geographic Society, Washington, DC; catalog #30352) this film explains how the Earth's surface is constantly changing through weather, erosion, earthquakes, and volcanoes). Afterward, she takes the students outside to the playground and constructs a chemical volcano as follows: She sets a soda bottle on the ground and builds up a mound of dirt around it so that only the top of the neck shows. She puts 1 tablespoon of liquid detergent in the bottle. She adds a few drops of food coloring, one cup of vinegar, and enough warm water to fill the bottle almost to the top. Very quickly, she adds 2 tablespoons of baking soda (that has been mixed with a little water) to the bottle. She invites students to discuss the similarities between their artificial volcano and the ones depicted in the video. Students record their discussions in their science journals. [Teaching Standards A, B, D; Content Standard D]

9:15–9:45 Writing Process

Facts on File: One group of students goes to the school library to research various books for facts about volcanoes. They collect information about the location of major volcanoes around the globe, as well as the damage that each volcano has done.

Journals: Several students have taken charge of monitoring the events surrounding Mount Kilauea in Hawaii as reported in the local newspaper. They record those events in their individual journals and compare notes on their individual interpretations.

Newspaper: A small group of students have designed a weekly newspaper that reports catastrophic events that happen around the world. They "assign" a reporter to each event, and he or she develops available information into an article.

Interviews: Some students have initiated a series of interviews with graduate students and professors at the University of California–Davis. The interviews center on recent volcanic eruptions in the South Pacific, a description and definition of pyroclastic flows, the science of predicting future volcanic eruptions, and volcanology as a career. [Teaching Standards B, D, E; Content Standards A, D, F, G]

9:45–10:30 Drama Time

Students are divided into four separate groups. Each group uses play houses and other models to create make-believe towns located near major volcanoes (Mount St. Helens, Kilauea, Mount Pinatubo). Each of these "towns" is assembled on a sheet of plywood along with a clay model of a volcano. Students create skits based on each of the three different types (Hawaiian, Strombolian, and Vulcanian) of volcanic eruptions and the effects on those towns. Students are invited to make videotapes of their skits. [Teaching Standards A, E; Content Standards B, F, G]

10:30–11:30 Required/Optional Activities

Group 1: Under the direction of the teacher's aide, students observe manipulation of a paraffin block on a hot plate to simulate the formation of a "hot spot" volcano, the type that formed the Hawaiian Islands over thousands of years.

Group 2: Students use the Internet (http://www.learner.org/k12) to contact working volcanologists to request information on the effects of volcanoes, eruption rates, and temperatures of different types of lava. The data will be collected in the form of charts and graphs.

Group 3: Students erect a "Graffiti Wall" outside the classroom and invite students from other classes to record information or research about volcanoes. Later, these ideas will be reconstructed in the form of a giant semantic web.

Group 4: After viewing the video *The Violent Earth* (National Geographic Society, Washington, DC; catalog #51234), students compose a book of adjectives and descriptive phrases that have been used to describe various volcanoes around the world.

Group 5: Students obtain the address of Hawaii Volcanoes National Park (P.O. Box 52, Hawaii National Park, HI 96718). They write to request the park's newspaper, descriptive brochures, and information on recent eruptions of Kilauea. They will later compare these data with information from library resources and newspaper clippings. [Teaching Standards B, D, E; Content Standards A, D, E, F, G]

11:30–12:00 Lunch

12:00–12:30 Sustained Silent Reading

Students obtain books from the collection that Gail offers. Books selected include *Earthquakes and Volcanoes* by Fiona Watt (Usborne, 1993), *Mountains and Volcanoes* by Barbara Taylor (Kingfisher, 1993), *Volcano and Earthquake* by Susanna Rose (Knopf, 1992), *Surtsey: The Newest Place on Earth* by Kathryn Lasky (Hyperion, 1992), and *Volcanoes* by Gregory Vogt (Watts, 1993). Several groups of two and three students have formed to share their selected books in cooperative reading groups. [Teaching Standards A, D; Content Standards A, G]

12:30–1:15 Teacher-Directed Activities

Opening: Gail decides to open the day's lesson with an anticipation guide. Using the book *Volcanoes* by Seymour Simon (Morrow, 1988), she creates the following set of statements that are presented to students before reading the book:

Before   After

_____   _____   1. Volcanoes happen all over the world.

_____   _____   2. More volcanoes happen in Hawaii than in any other state.

_____   _____   3. A volcano is the most destructive natural disaster in the world.

_____   _____   4. Volcanoes always occur along tectonic plates.

_____   _____   5. Volcanoes are rare occurrences.

Gail provides the students with a duplicated copy of the guide and invites them to record "True" or "False" in the "Before" column, depending on their personal beliefs.

Class Discussion: The class discusses the responses made on individual anticipation guides. They voice agreements and disagreements and record ideas on the chalkboard. Gail invites students to make predictions about the book.

Selected Reading: Gail reads the book *Volcanoes* to the class. Before reading, she invites students to listen for statements or information that may confirm or modify their responses to the anticipation guide statements recorded earlier. She also stops periodically throughout the reading and invites students to change their original predictions based on data in the book.

Closure: Gail invites students to assemble in small groups and complete the "After" column of the anticipation guide (based on the information learned in the book, students record "True" or "False" in the space in front of each statement). Later, she encourages students to share reasons for their responses and any changes they may have made in their original recordings. Gail encourages students to confirm their ideas through additional reading in other pieces of literature. [Teaching Standards A, C; Content Standards A, E, G]

1:15–1:35 Storytelling or Read Aloud

The students all gather on the large "Reading Rug" in the back of the classroom to listen to Gail read the book *What If...The Earth* by Steve Parker (Franklin Watts, 1995). Afterward, students discuss volcanoes and lithospheric plates (this discussion will form the basis for extending activities related to other natural changes on the surface of the Earth, such as earthquakes, glaciers, and erosion). [Teaching Standards A, B, C, E; Content Standards A, B, D, G]

1:35–2:10 Art and Music

The art teacher, Mr. Muñoz, has posted a large sheet of newsprint in the school cafeteria. He invites students, in small groups, to create a large mural of the events that would happen during and immediately after a volcanic eruption. Mr. Muñoz has shared slides of Diego Rivera's murals that have been painted on public buildings throughout Mexico (he will later extend this into a series of geography and history lessons on the land and culture of Mexico). [Teaching Standards A, B, D; Content Standards F, G]

2:10–2:40 Self-Selected Activities

Group 1: A small group of students creates models of each of the four different types of volcanoes: shield volcano (Mauna Loa), cinder cone volcano (El Misti), strato-volcano (Mount Fuji), and dome volcano (Mount St. Helens). The models will be displayed in the school library.

Group 2: Students construct models of the two basic types of lava (*pahoehoe* and *aa*) using modeling clay and photographs from various books. They will display them in the classroom with appropriate labels.

Group 3: Students create an extended time line of the major events related to the continuing eruption of Kilauea volcano in Hawaii. They select events reported on television, the Internet, and in the newspaper.

Group 4: Students write letters to university students at the University of California–Berkeley requesting a personal visit. They invite the college students to share information learned during a recent course on volcanology.

Group 5: Two small groups of students each put together bibliographies of current trade books related to "The Changing Earth." They will share these bibliographies with teachers in other classes. [Teaching Standards A, B, C, D, E; Content Standards A, D, E, F, G]

2:40–3:00 Responding to Literature

Students finish reading the book *Volcano: The Eruption and Healing of Mount St. Helens* by Patricia Lauber (Aladdin, 1986). The class has been divided into three separate groups. The first discusses the similarities between Mount St. Helens and a volcano erupting in the South Pacific. The second group develops a "story map" that outlines the major elements of the book in a graphic representation. The third group summarizes the major points of the book in the form of a newspaper article to be included in the class newspaper, *Earth Watch*. [Teaching Standards B, D; Content Standards D, F, G]

3:00–3:15 Daily Closure

Gail divides the class into "teams" of three students each. The teams discuss some of the items they learned during the course of the day, items to work on in following days, and those items for which they would still like to obtain additional information. Each team's recorder shares some of the discussion with the entire class. Gail encourages students to share their ideas with parents upon their return home. [Teaching Standards B, C, D, E; Content Standards A, F]

Changing Science Instruction

Gail and thousands of other teachers around the country have discovered that the National Science Education Standards offer multiple opportunities for classroom teachers to share the joy and excitement of science education with greater numbers of students. This "marriage" facilitates science instruction (particularly for those who are less than comfortable with their scientific background) and helps students view science as a process of discovery and exploration, rather than one of memorization and regurgitation.

The standards, in concert with literature-based instruction, are generating some remarkable changes in the ways that science is taught and the ways in which it is learned. These changes are summarized in Table 2.3 below.

Table 2.3.
Changing Emphases

Less Emphasis On	More Emphasis On
Treating all students alike and responding to the group as a whole	Understanding and responding to individual student's interests, strengths, experiences, and needs
Rigidly following curriculum	Selecting and adapting curriculum
Focusing on student acquisition of information	Focusing on student understanding and use of scientific knowledge, ideas, and inquiry processes
Presenting scientific knowledge through lecture, text, and demonstration	Guiding students in active and extended scientific inquiry
Asking for recitation of acquired knowledge	Providing opportunities for scientific discussion and debate among students
Testing students for factual information at the end of the unit or chapter	Continuously assessing student understanding
Maintaining responsibility and authority	Sharing responsibility for learning with students
Supporting competition	Supporting a classroom community with cooperation, shared responsibility, and respect
Working alone	Working with other teachers to enhance the science program

From the National Academy of Sciences, *National Science Education Standards* (Washington, D.C.: National Academy of Sciences, 1996), 30–52, 121–71.

Literature-based instruction not only offers students unique opportunities to process and practice "hands-on" science, it also provides teachers with integrative strategies and activities that enhance science education in all curricular areas. In addition, this method of instruction assists students in drawing realistic parallels between classroom enterprises and events and circumstances outside the classroom. In short, literature-based science instruction can aid students in understanding the relevancy of science to their everyday lives.

Chapter 3

How to Use This Book

Welcome to an exciting voyage! The following chapters contain a host of activities and processes designed for some of the best trade books in elementary science. I have selected these books because they are appropriate to the science curriculum, adaptable to all elementary grades (K–6) and ability ranges (high–low), and useful in promoting a better understanding of natural disasters. Included are a variety of award-winning books, fresh new literature, and "classics" recommended by teachers and children's librarians from throughout the country. The featured books also include factual literature, activity books, and narrative stories in a wide variety of genres. In short, there's something for everyone!

The children's literature selections have been organized around seven natural disaster concepts—volcanoes, earthquakes, floods and tsunamis, hurricanes, tornadoes, avalanches and landslides, and storms. (Note: Also included in Appendix D is a listing of Web sites and literature related to other natural occurrences.) It was my desire to demonstrate the wide variety of children's literature available for any study of natural disasters. Undoubtedly, you will discover that most of these books can be used across the length and breadth of the science curriculum.

The literature selections included within this book reflect a range of reading levels. You should feel free to select and use literature that best meets the needs and abilities of your students in addition to promoting specific science concepts. An "energized" science curriculum will include literature selections throughout its length and breadth. You will discover innumerable opportunities for developing, expanding, and teaching all the science standards using the literature in these pages. In that regard, remember that the readability or difficulty level of a single book should not determine if or how it will be used; rather, the emphasis should be on whether students are interested and motivated to pursue literature-related activities that promote learning in a supportive and holistic science curriculum.

Each featured book includes a host of potential activities and processes. It is not necessary to use all of these activities. Rather, you and your students should decide on the activities that best serve the needs of the science program and of students themselves. Undoubtedly, you will discover activities that can be used individually, in small groups, in large groups, or as a whole class. So too, will you find a host of activities in every curricular area, activities that will help you extend and expand the science program across the elementary curriculum. Science, social studies, art, music, physical education, reading, and language arts are all reflected in these activities, helping students see the relevance of scientific inquiry and discovery in terms of the entire education program.

You also will discover many different ways of individualizing your science program through these suggested activities and projects. Providing students with opportunities to make activity selections within the context of a work of literature can be a powerful and energizing component of your science program. When teachers give youngsters such opportunities, their appreciation of science and their interest in learning important concepts increases tremendously.

As students become involved in the various trade books and their accompanying activities, I suggest that you guide them in researching or developing other activities based on classroom dynamics and on teaching-learning styles. For learning to be meaningful, it must have relevance. I encourage you and your students to make these activities your own. Add to them, adapt them, and allow students to help you design additional activities, extensions, and projects that will challenge them, arouse their natural curiosity, and create a dynamic learning environment.

Implementing a Literature-Based Program

Teaching science with trade books is not necessarily an "all-or-nothing" proposition. That is, it is not necessary to use a single trade book for a full lesson or full day. You have several options in terms of how you can present a book or series of books to your class, how much you want them to dominate your daily curriculum, and how involved you and your students want to be. Obviously, your level of comfort with literature-based teaching and the scope and sequence of your classroom or district science curriculum may determine the degree to which you use these books. Here are some options for you to consider:

1. Introduce a single book and provide students with a variety of selected activities (for that book) for one day.

2. Teach a unit built on a combination of several related books.

3. Design a thematic unit based on selected pieces of literature within a specific science standard.

4. Design a thematic unit based on selected pieces of literature within a specific science discipline.

5. Design a thematic unit based on selected pieces of literature within a specific science concept area.

6. Use the activities for one or two books during an entire day and follow up with the regular curriculum in succeeding days.

7. Use a book or series of books as a follow-up to information and data presented in a textbook or curriculum guide.

8. Provide students with literature-related activities as independent work. This can be done upon completion of lessons in the regular textbook.

9. Teach cooperatively with a colleague and present a self-designed unit to both classes at the same time (this can be done with two classes at the same grade or two different classes, each at a different grade level).

10. Use a book or group of books intermittently over the span of several weeks.

Any number of factors may determine how you use these books. It is safe to say that there is no ideal way to implement literature into your classroom plans. The listing above is only a partial collection of ideas. The dictates of your own particular teaching situation and personal experience, as well as your students' needs, may suggest other possibilities or alternatives to this register of ideas.

Throughout this book a variety of Internet sites have been suggested as positive learning extensions of the science of natural disasters and for specific trade books. As you know, the Internet is dynamic and constantly changing. The Web sites listed were current and accurate as of the writing of this book. Please be aware that some may change, others may be eliminated, and new ones will be added to the various search engines that you use at school or home. If you discover a "dead" site or a new Web site on natural disasters that other teachers might enjoy, please feel free to contact me at **afrederi@gte.net** or via my Web site at **www.afredericks.com**.

Part 2

Activities and Processes

Chapter 4
Volcanoes

June 15, 1991

After more than 600 years of inactivity, Mount Pinatubo rumbled back to life in 1991. In early March, local residents felt small earthquakes. Volcanologists set up special monitoring devices around the ancient volcano. Over the next few months, the earthquakes intensified, sulfur dioxide gas emissions increased, and small ash explosions occurred on a regular, but unpredictable, basis. Large explosions occurred in early June, and tens of thousands of residents in neighboring villages and towns—as well as the entire population of Clark Air Force Base—were evacuated from the area.

On June 15, the volcano blew its top! A mushroom cloud of ash 240 miles wide and 21 miles high jetted into the atmosphere. The volume of ash was enormous, covering cities and towns with feet (not inches) of thick wet ashfall. There was so much ash in the air that light from the sun was completely blocked for days. Scientists later recorded this volcanic explosion as one of the most intense of the twentieth century.

The Science of Volcanoes

According to scientists, Earth is made of a thin layer of hard rock (the lithosphere) that rests on a thick layer of partially melted rock (the asthenosphere). The lithosphere is broken into several plates (known as tectonic plates). Most of the world's volcanoes are found along the edges of those plates where the crust is weak and where magma can push upward.

A volcano is any opening in the crust of the Earth through which molten rock (magma), gases, ash, and rock fragments erupt. Volcanoes start when rock inside the Earth melts, creating a gas that mixes with the magma. The magma then rises to the Earth's surface because it is lighter than the solid rock around it. When magma exits the Earth, it is called lava.

Lava may come from the top of a volcano or from its sides. As magma rises from the Earth's interior, it collects in an area known as a magma reservoir, or chamber, just below the surface. Enlarged cracks, known as pipes, often lead from the magma reservoir. There may be many pipes, but not all reach the surface. Those that open to the surface are called vents or rifts. Some vents lie inside a deep hollow known as a crater (often the top of a volcano). Others are scattered along the sides of the volcano. Occasionally, old vents close and new ones form. Often, scientists don't know where a new vent will open to spill lava across the landscape.

Volcanoes are classified as active (those that are currently erupting or have recently erupted, such as Kilauea in Hawaii), dormant (those that have not erupted for some time but still show signs of some activity, such as Mount Rainier in Washington), and extinct (those that have not erupted for some time, with no signs of activity, such as Crater Lake in Oregon). Volcanoes also are classified according to their shape. A shield volcano (such as Mauna Loa in Hawaii) has broad gentle slopes. A composite volcano or strato-volcano (Mount Fuji in Japan) is made up of mixed layers of cinders and lava flow. A cinder cone volcano (El Misti in Peru) looks like an upside-down ice cream cone with very steep sides. A dome volcano (Lassen Peak in California) has thick, slow-moving lava that forms a steep-sided dome shape.

Dear Katie, The Volcano Is a Girl

Jean Craighead George

New York: Hyperion Books, 1998

Summary

Katie and her grandmother get into a friendly argument about Kilauea volcano in Hawaii. The grandmother believes that the volcano is a geophysical phenomenon caused by hot spots in the Earth's crust. Katie argues that the volcano is really Pele, the Hawaiian goddess of fire. Each presents her view, and in the end each is proven correct. This is a great story to share with students because it brings a distinctive human quality to the study of volcanoes. The artist traveled to Hawaii under a special grant to create the watercolors that add a mystical quality to this engaging story. (Note: There are some factual misinterpretations on one page of this book; see Activity 7 below. These errors do not detract from the quality of the book as a whole, however).

Science Education Standards

The questions and activities in this section can be used to support teaching of the following content standards.

Science As Inquiry

Abilities necessary to do scientific inquiry

Physical Science

Properties and changes of properties in matter

Earth and Space Science

Structure of the Earth system

Science in Personal and Social Perspectives

Changes in environments
Natural hazards

Critical Thinking Questions

1. Which of the two characters do you think is correct?

2. How did the illustrations contribute to your understanding of the legend of Pele?

3. Would you like to visit Kileaua in Hawaii?

4. What would you like to tell the girl at the end of the story?

5.   How is this book similar to or different from other books on volcanoes?

Activities

1.   Invite college students from a local university to share specially prepared lessons on volcanoes. Additionally, invite students majoring in geology at the university to share their expertise with the class. Invite your students to interview the college students and gather that data together in specially prepared notebooks or journals.

2.   Students may wish to log on to various Web sites to learn more about our fiftieth state. Here are some to get them started:

> http://www.hawaii.net/cgi-bin/hhp?
>
> http://www.geobop.com/Eco/HI.htm
>
> http://www.mhpcc.edu/tour/Tour.html
>
> http://www.maui.net/~leodio/higuide.html
>
> http://tqjunior.advanced.org/3502/

3.   Students may wish to create their own chemical volcano with the following activity. Cut a piece of cardboard into the shape of a cone (this cone should be able to fit over a small jar, such as a baby food jar). The cone should have a small hole in the top. Place the jar on a cookie sheet. (Note: The following steps need to be done very rapidly.) Hold the cone in one hand. With the other hand pour half a cup of hydrogen peroxide into the jar. Follow that quickly with half a teaspoon of quick-rising yeast. Stir the mixture thoroughly (and quickly), then place the cone back over the jar. You may need to stir the mixture again to continue the "eruption." (Note: This activity should be done by an adult only.)

  Students will note that the mixture of yeast and hydrogen peroxide results in a lot of foam, some steam, and a little hissing. This chemical reaction also will produce some degree of heat (students will be able to feel the heat on the sides of the jar). This is an example of an exothermic chemical reaction, one that generates heat. This reaction is similar to the heat an erupting volcano generates.

4.   Ask students to log on to the Web site http://volcano.und.nodak.edu. This site offers students opportunities to e-mail working volcanologists, keep up to date on the latest volcanic eruptions, and discover how volcanoes work. (Note: Teachers can also get complete lesson plans on volcanoes at this site.)

5.   Encourage students to post a large map of the world on one wall of the classroom. Have them indicate the locations of volcanoes around the world with pushpins or sticky dots. (Students may need to conduct some preliminary research on various Web sites or in several books for the necessary information.) Where are most of the world's active volcanoes located?

6.   Have students write to the Hawaii Visitors Bureau (2270 Kalakaua Ave., Suite 801, Honolulu, HI 96815) to obtain information and brochures about the state. Students may also wish to contact a local travel agency for posters, brochures, and travel information.

7. There are some misrepresentations of factual information on one page of the book (the pages are unnumbered). Turn to the page early in the book that shows large waves inundating a coastal town. Present students with the following four statements from the book and ask them to access various Web sites or use other children's literature to correct these misrepresentations:

> "Before a volcanic eruption there are violent earthquakes." (Earthquakes may occur before an eruption, but this is not always the case. Kileaua volcano, for example, has been erupting continuously since 1984 with only a few accompanying earthquakes.)

> "…earthquakes crack open the ocean floor." (Sometimes earthquakes will crack the ocean floor, but not always. They also occur on land, sometimes causing visible cracks, but sometimes this does not occur.)

> "…earthquakes create…tidal waves." (From a scientific viewpoint, the author is referring to tsunamis, or harbor waves. The term "tidal wave" is a misnomer. Also, not all underwater earthquakes produce these waves—only about 1 in 10.)

> "…tidal waves…carry away cliffs, beaches, and mountainsides." (This occurs extremely rarely. Most tsunamis result in an inundation of coastal areas by large waves or tidal bores. The damage is to homes, buildings, and other structures. Most significant is the loss of life.)

8. If possible, invite an oceanographer or geologist from a local college or university to visit your classroom. Invite her or him to explain the science of volcanoes—those on land or those underwater.

9. Have students create a readers theatre script about the communication between the grandmother and the young girl. They may wish to produce their skit or play for other classes in the school.

10. Students may wish to learn more about the Hawaiian legend of Pele. The following Web sites will provide them with valuable and interesting information:

> http://www.nps.gov/havo/pele.htm
>
> http://alohaweb.com/Pele/synopopsis.html
>
> http://www.hitrade.com/2Kane_Pele.html
>
> http://www.coffeetimes.com/pele.htm

11. The following Web sites provide students with the most up-to-date information on Kilauea volcano, including its current eruption and various views of the volcano:

> http://wwwhvo.wr.usgs.gov/kilauea
>
> http://bolcano.und.nodak.edu.vwdocs/vwlessons/curr_volc.html
>
> http://www.soest.Hawaii.edu/GG/hcv.html
>
> http://wwwhvo.wr.usgs.gov

12.   Students may wish to visit a Web site that has the "Top 101 Frequently Asked Questions" about volcanoes. At http://volcano.und.edu/vwdocs/ask_a.html is a list of questions asked by students across the country and answered by some of the world's leading volcanologists. Ask students to review the listed questions and determine if there is a volcano question they have that is not represented on the listing.

13.   Here is a brief listing of some other books about Hawaii that students may enjoy. Check them out at your school or public library. They may also be located through any on-line bookstore:

   Feeney, Stephanie. *A is for Aloha*. (Honolulu: University of Hawaii Press, 1985).

   Fradin, Dennis. *Hawaii (From Sea to Shining Sea)*. (New York: Children's Press, 1994).

   Nunes, Susan. *To Find the Way*. (Honolulu: University of Hawaii Press, 1992).

   Rumford, James. *The Island-Below-the-Star*. (Boston: Houghton Mifflin, 1998).

   Siy, Alexandria. *Hawaiian Islands*. (New York: Dillon Press, 1991).

   Staub, Frank. *Children of Hawaii*. (Minneapolis: Carolrhoda Books, 1998).

   Wardlaw, Lee. *Punia and the King of Sharks*. (New York: Dial, 1997).

Surtsey: The Newest Place on Earth

Kathryn Lasky

New York: Hyperion Books, 1992

Summary

Early on a November morning in 1963, a volcanic eruption off the coast of Iceland broke through the waves and began to create a brand new island. Belching fire and smoke into the sky, the volcano built layer upon layer of lava on itself and rose toward the sun. Scientists were stunned and awed by the incredible scene unfolding before them—land was being created. In a compelling and mesmerizing book, the author and photographer present readers with one of the most fascinating stories of volcanic activity ever to appear in a children's book. Not only is this book a great research tool, it also will be an important read-aloud book for classroom use.

Science Education Standards

The questions and activities in this section can be used to support teaching of the following content standards.

Science As Inquiry

Abilities necessary to do scientific inquiry
Understanding about scientific inquiry

Earth and Space Science

Properties of Earth materials
Changes in Earth and sky
Structure of the Earth system
Earth's history

Science in Personal and Social Perspectives

Science and technology in local challenges
Natural hazards

History and Nature of Science

Science as a human endeavor

Critical Thinking Questions

1. What did you find so amazing about the "birth" of Surtsey?

2. How is Surtsey similar to other volcanoes you know about?

3. What was the most important discovery on Surtsey?

4. Would you enjoy being a scientist on Surtsey?

5. What other types of animals do you think will find their way to Surtsey?

6. What will Surtsey look like in 50 years?

Activities

1. Invite students to initiate and maintain an "Earth Watch Newspaper," a collection of stories about new and continuing volcanoes around the world. Encourage students to report their findings (to your class or another) periodically.

2. Challenge individual students to create an advertisement (written or oral) for a new volcano (such as Surtsey). Ask class members to describe the features that would be most necessary in the promotion (i.e., the sale) of an active, inactive, or dormant volcano.

3. Encourage students to work in small groups to create dioramas of the Surtsey area before and immediately after the volcanic eruption. Other groups of students may wish to create "Before" and "After" dioramas of selected volcanic eruptions from around the world. Provide opportunities for students to discuss their creations and share them with students in other classes.

4. Students may enjoy creating another type of volcanic eruption. (Note: This activity must be done outdoors for maximum results and safety. Teachers of younger students can use this as a demonstration.) Place a 20-ounce glass bottle on the ground and build up a mound of dirt around the sides so that only the top of the bottle is showing. Place 1 tablespoon of liquid detergent into the bottle. Add a few drops of red food coloring to the bottle. Pour in 1 cup of vinegar and add enough warm water to fill the bottle almost to the top. Very rapidly, add 2 tablespoons of baking soda that has been mixed with a little water. Stand back and watch your volcano "erupt."

    In this activity, the baking soda reacts with the vinegar to create a chemical reaction (carbon dioxide is produced). Because carbon dioxide gas is heavier than air, it pushes the air out of the bottle. The detergent in the bottle helps create more bubbles, and the food coloring makes the "eruption" more spectacular.

5. Additional information and pertinent data about the island of Surtsey can be obtained on the following Web sites. Although most of the information on these sites is geared for adult readers, students may wish to access them to obtain additional data about this remarkable island beyond what is explained in the book.

    http://volcano.und.nodak.edu/vwdocs/volc_images/Europe_west_asia/
      surtsey.html

    http://denali.gsfc.nasa.gov/research/garvin/surtsey.html

    http://www.south.is/surtsey.html

    http://www.geophy.Washington.edu/People/Students/throstho/
      Vinna/surt.../nytt_surtsey.htm

6. To reinforce how folktales are passed down from generation to generation, divide the class into several groups and invite each group to create its own original folktale. Encourage each group to record their tale and preserve it in a special location. Several months later, ask group members to recall the specifics of their folktale, then play the recording of their original story. Discuss the changes that occurred between the two tellings. Let students know that these changes are a normal and natural part of storytelling that give folktales their special flavor and design.

7. As part of a class discussion, invite students to record important developments in the "birth" of Surtsey on a time line. This can be a sheet of newsprint posted along one wall of the classroom or an extending strip of adding-machine tape attached to the wall of the hallway. Here's an example:

———/———/———/———/———/———/———/———/———/

11/14/63   11/20/63   12/63   1/64   8/64   6/65   1967   1968   1970

8. Have students create several different examples of Surtsey from its "birth" to its present-day shape. Using the photographs and descriptions in the book, encourage students to create four or five replicas of Surtsey using the following recipe for dough.

> 1 cup flour
> ½ cup salt
> ⅓ cup water
>
> Mix the flour and salt. Add the water, a little at a time. Squeeze the dough until it is smooth. Form it into one of the shapes of Surtsey during its development. Let it air dry or bake it at 225 degrees for about 60 minutes. Paint with tempera paints. (Note: This recipe is sufficient for one "volcano." Adjust it according to the number of volcanoes students wish to construct.)

9. Students can obtain information about Iceland, its people, its history and customs, and its flags by accessing the following Web sites. Ask small groups of students to gather information from these sites and from brochures or flyers from a neighborhood travel agency. Encourage them to assemble the data together into a kid-oriented brochure on Iceland.

http://www.interknowledge.com/Iceland.main.htm

http://fotw.digibel.be/flags/is.html

10. Students may enjoy reading other books by award-winning author Kathryn Lasky. Here is a small sampling of additional titles available in school or public libraries or through various on-line bookstores:

> *Beyond the Burning Time*
>
> *Cloud Eyes*
>
> *Days of the Dead*
>
> *Dreams of the Golden Country*
>
> *The Gates of the Wind*

11. Invite students to create a bulletin board display describing how different types of islands are created. Some are created as a result of volcanic activity, some are created as the result of geologic forces over time, and others are created through continental drift or a movement of tectonic plates. Encourage students to provide illustrations of several different islands from around the world. Additional information on island formation can be obtained on the following Web sites:

    http://windows.ivv.nasa.gov/cgi-bin/tour_def/Earth/interior/
        island_formation.html

    http://www.lcsc.edu/GEOL100-cip/Hawaii_illustrations.htm

12. Have several groups of students blow up small balloons. Mix equal parts of liquid starch and water together until the starch is dissolved. Then soak newspaper strips (2 inches wide by 8 inches long) in the mixture and layer them over the balloons. When dry, students may use tempera paints to create the continents and oceans of the world. Have them indicate (with stickers or paint) the locations of major volcanoes around the world. Students may also wish to position important volcanic islands on their home-made globes, too.

13. Have students imagine that they are the person living in the scientists' hut on the island. Encourage them to create a series of letters or postcards that they might send home to their family and friends about the "happenings" on the island. What new plants or animals are visiting the island? Has there been any recent volcanic activity? What types of scientists are visiting the island? What have they been able to discover? Be sure to provide sufficient opportunities for students to share and discuss their communiqués with each other.

14. Ask students to read *50 Simple Things Kids Can Do to Save the Earth* (Kansas City, KS: Andrews and McMeel, 1990). Invite them to develop a plan that will ensure the island of Surtsey remains forever unspoiled. Small groups of students may wish to create a list of "Dos" and "Don'ts" on the preservation of Surtsey.

The Village of Round and Square Houses

Ann Grifalconi

Boston: Little, Brown, 1986

Summary

In the Cameroons of Central Africa exists an isolated village named Tos. In that village the women live in round houses, and the men live in square houses. The story of how this came to be is told through the eyes of a young girl as she shares a beautiful legend about a community and its people. This book is not only about villagers but about how a natural phenomenon shaped and altered their lives. This is an ideal read-aloud book for an entire class or a lead book for a lesson of the relationships that exist between geological forces and human beings.

Science Education Standards

The questions and activities in this section can be used to support teaching of the following content standards.

Science As Inquiry

Abilities necessary to do scientific inquiry

Earth and Space Science

Changes in Earth and sky
Structure of the Earth system
Earth's history

Science in Personal and Social Perspectives

Changes in the environment; Science and technology in local challenges
Natural hazards

History and Nature of Science

Science as a human endeavor

Critical Thinking Questions

1. How is the village of Tos similar to the town or city where you live?

2. What did you enjoy most about life in the village of Tos (before the volcano eruption)?

3. How is the narrator similar to you, a family member, or one of your friends?

4. How do such natural events as erupting volcanoes and earthquakes change the way people live?

5.   How would your life change if a volcano erupted nearby?

Activities

1.   Ask students to complete some of the "sentence stems" below:

> "If I lived in near a volcano, I would…"
>
> "If a volcano erupted in my neighborhood, I would…"
>
> "I think volcanoes are…"
>
> "The most dangerous part about living in a volcanically active region would be…"
>
> "I would like to learn more about…"

2.   Obtain copies of several different telephone books. Have students browse through the yellow pages of the telephone books and locate items or services that might be needed in the event of a local volcanic eruption (e.g., telephone service, carpet cleaning, home repair). Students may wish to create their own special "Volcano Yellow Pages," listing services that are not normally found in most municipal phone books (e.g., lava removal, air purification).

3.   Ask students to create a play or readers theatre adaptation of this story. Encourage students to divide the story into "chunks" and to assign speaking parts to the major and minor characters in the story. Examples and directions for constructing readers theatre scripts can be found in one or more of the following books: *Frantic Frogs and Other Frankly Fractured Folktales for Readers Theatre*, *Tadpole Tales and Other Totally Terrific Treats for Readers Theatre*, and *Silly Salamanders and Other Slightly Stupid Stories for Readers Theatre* (all by Anthony D. Fredericks).

4.   Provide students with copies of different newspapers from selected cities around the country. (Many metropolitan areas have newsstands where different newspapers from various cities are sold.) Have students look through the newspapers for articles, information, or data relating to eruptions of volcanoes. (At the time of this writing, Mount Kilauea volcano in Hawaii is in a constant process of eruption.) Ask students to cut out those articles and assemble them into an ongoing journal. Index cards with a brief summary of the date, location, and events surrounding an eruption can be posted around a large wall map for others to read.

5.   Obtain a copy of the volcano books listed in Appendix A. Provide opportunities for students to read these books. Afterward, invite students to compare the photographs in *The Village of Round and Square Houses* with volcano photos in other books. Encourage students to categorize the photos from various sources according to one of the four types of volcanoes: shield, cinder cone, composite, and dome. Ask students to categorize the volcano in *The Village of Round and Square Houses* into one of the four groups.

6.   Encourage students to create a sequel to *The Village of Round and Square Houses*. What does the village look like in 5 years, 10 years, 50 years? Does the volcano erupt again? Is life in the village the same or different from that portrayed in the book? Plan

to provide sufficient opportunities for students to share their stories. Encourage students to collect appropriate data about this country and create a special bulletin board display for the classroom.

7. Students may be interested in gathering information about the country of Cameroon. Have them access one or more of the following Web sites:

> http://www.odci.gov/cia/publications/factbook/cm.html
>
> http://www.Theodora.com/flags/cm.gif
>
> http://media.maps.com/Magellan/Images/CAMERO-W1.gif

8. Invite students to take an imaginary trip to Cameroon. Encourage them to keep journals about their travels. They may wish to include information such as location, sites, weather, customs, food, and the people. Ask students to note both similarities and differences between the United States and Cameroon.

9. Have students collect newspaper and magazine articles about Cameroon. Students may wish to assemble these into an attractive notebook or scrapbook for display in the school library. Additional information on this country (and surrounding countries) can be obtained at the following Web sites:

> http://hyperion.advanced.org/16645/
>
> http://www.hmnet.com/Africa/1africa.html
>
> http://www.geographica.com/indx06.htm

10. If possible, obtain a copy of either of the following two videos, which are available from the National Geographic Society (see Appendix C): *This Changing Planet* (catalog #30352) or *The Violent Earth* (catalog #51234). Provide opportunities for students to share the similarities and differences between the volcanoes shown in the film(s) and the volcano described in the book.

11. The following Web site has an incredible collection of photos, images, animations, and videos of various volcanoes from around the world. If possible, arrange a time to share some of the incredible information available on this site: http://www.yahooligans. com/Downloader/Pictures/School_Bell/Science_Technology/Geology/Volcanoes/

12. Have students present a mini lesson to another class on the effect of volcanoes on the surrounding environment or on human and animal communities. Students can present the lesson in person or on videotape.

13. Ask students to gather information from the school or public library. Encourage them to assemble a booklet or poster titled Volcano Records—a Compendium of Records about Volcanoes Around the World. The following suggestions may help to get students started; suggest that they find records for volcanoes both in the United States or North America and worldwide:

> Tallest volcano
>
> Shortest volcano
>
> Oldest active volcano

Most active volcano

Most continuously active volcano

Most violent volcanic eruption

Most destructive volcano

14.   Ask each student in the class to "adopt" a volcano from somewhere in the world. Each student must provide a biography of her or his volcano, including the height and activity of the adoptee, recent rumblings, and other vital information and statistics. Provide regular opportunities for students to share their adoptees with other members of the class.

Volcano: The Eruption and Healing of Mount St. Helens

Patricia Lauber

New York: Aladdin Books, 1986

Summary

In May of 1980, one of this country's most violent volcanic eruptions occurred in Washington. Mount St. Helens, quiet for hundreds of years, literally blew her top. Tons of smoke and ash were propelled into the atmosphere, dozens of people were killed, an entire ecosystem was virtually wiped out, and the local environment was transformed forever. This book is both eloquent and mesmerizing. With an eye toward scientific accuracy and the skill of a storyteller, the author shares a story that is both gripping and incredible. Every unit on volcanic activity should include this book; it is one that will stimulate and captivate readers young and old.

Science Education Standards

The questions and activities in this section can be used to support teaching of the following content standards.

Science As Inquiry

Abilities necessary to do scientific inquiry
Understanding about scientific inquiry

Earth and Space Science

Changes in Earth and sky
Structure of the Earth system

Science in Personal and Social Perspectives

Changes in environment
Natural hazards

History and Nature of Science

Science as a human endeavor
History of science

Critical Thinking Questions

1.   What did you find so amazing about the eruption of Mount St. Helens?

2.   Why was there so much destruction?

3. What questions would you like to ask the scientists who study Mount St. Helens?

4. What questions would you like to ask the author?

5. How can people prepare for future volcanic eruptions in the United States?

6. What do you think Mount St. Helens will look like in 50 years? 100 years?

Activities

1. Before reading the book with students, provide them with photographs of Mount St. Helens before the eruption. Have them imagine what the mountain must have looked like after the eruption and encourage them to each draw an illustration of how they think the mountain may have looked after the eruption. Later, invite students to compare their predictions with the actual photos in the book. What differences do they note?

2. Ask students to imagine that they are a volcano. Have them write their biography from this perspective in journals. Encourage students to write about the following questions: Why did they erupt? What did they feel before and after the eruption? What triggered the eruption? How did the eruption effect the environment in the immediate vicinity? Afterward, students may wish to create an illustration of themselves (as volcanoes) to share with the class.

3. Have students research other books about volcanoes. Students may wish to choose a volcano (e.g., Mount Fuji) to compare and contrast with Mount St. Helens.

4. Ask small groups of students to write fictional stories about how they were effected when Mount St. Helens erupted. What were some of the effects of the volcano's eruption on their daily lives? How did they survive? What did they do afterward? Provide opportunities for students to share their creations with the class.

5. Demonstrate the gas pressure that builds up inside of volcanoes by shaking up a bottle of warm soda and then taking the cap off (use caution). Invite students to compare what they observed with the eruption of Mount St. Helens. Students may wish to discuss how the soda compares with the magma of Mount St. Helens.

6. Divide the class into groups of "scientists." Invite each group to chart the specific eruptions of Mount St. Helens on a piece of poster board. Students may wish to include the date of the eruption, what caused the eruption, what type of eruption it was, and what the effects were. Invite each group to give a presentation of their findings.

7. Generate a class discussion on how the eruption of Mount St. Helens had an affect on the food chain of the surrounding area. Encourage students to discuss questions such as the following: How did the avalanches and mudslides affect the food chain? What are some ways that the vegetation was able to rejuvenate after the eruption? How were some animals able to escape harm during the eruption? Invite students to create individual journals to record their discussions.

8. Ask students to compare and contrast the environment immediately following the eruption to the environment two years after the eruption. Encourage students to take on the roles of news reporters and "interview" the plants and animals in the region about the processes they experienced during this transition phase.

9. Ask students to create a Venn diagram of important information recorded in *Surtsey: The Newest Place on Earth* and in *Volcano: The Eruption and Healing of Mount St. Helens*. Encourage them to describe the similarities and differences between these two volcanic eruptions. Plan sufficient time for students to discuss their findings and interpretations.

10. The following Web site provides current and up-to-the-minute news about erupting volcanoes around the world: http://headlines.yahoo.com/Full_Coverage/Yahooligans/EarthquakesVolcanoes. Invite students to log on to this site on a regular basis. They may wish to assemble data and information and make regular reports (via the intercom system or a classroom newspaper) on the status of selected volcanoes around the world. Updates on currently erupting volcanoes can also be included in the report(s).

11. The following Web sites provide students with information about different types of volcanoes including how they form, where they form, and their eruption rates. Plan time for students to access one or more of these sites. Students may wish to share the information with other classes via presentations or reports:

> http://library.thinkquest.org/17457
>
> http://www.learner.org/exhibits/volcanoes/
>
> http://www.pbs.org/wnet/savageearth/volcanoes/index.html
>
> http://clam.Rutgers.edu/~vlopez/geology/index.html

Volcanoes

Seymour Simon

New York: Morrow, 1988

Summary

In this extraordinary book, readers have the opportunity to explore some of the most amazing and majestic volcanoes in the world. They learn that volcanoes, for all their fiery splendor and famed destruction, also produce new mountains, new islands, and new soil. As is usual with many of the author's books, this is an unforgettable journey for any young scientist or volcanologist. The writing is direct and provides comprehensible explanations of complex geological events. Readers of any age will find this book a "must have" for the study of volcanoes around the world.

Science Education Standards

The questions and activities in this section can be used to support teaching of the following content standards.

Science As Inquiry

Understanding about scientific inquiry

Earth and Space Science

Changes in Earth and sky

Science in Personal and Social Perspectives

Changes in environments
Natural hazards

Critical Thinking Questions

1. What was the most amazing thing you learned in this book?

2. Did the author change your mind about what a volcano does?

3. What do you think would be the consequences if a volcano erupted in our local area?

4. Which of the volcanoes mentioned in the book would you like to visit? Why?

5. Should people fear volcanoes?

Activities

1. Some students may be interested in investigating the myths and legends of volcanoes throughout history. How do those stories and tales compare with what modern science knows about volcanoes today?

2. Obtain some potting soil and volcanic ash, which can be obtained through science supply companies (e.g., Hubbard Scientific, P.O. Box 104, Northbrook, IL 60065, 800-323-8368; The Institute for Earth Education, P.O. Box 288, Warrenville, IL 60555, 509-395-2299; or Scott Resources, P.O. Box 2121F, Fort Collins, CO 80522, 800-289-9299). Mix different amounts of ash with potting soil. Fill several compartments of an egg carton with the different mixtures and plant several vegetable seeds in each compartment. Encourage students to compare the relative growth rates of the vegetables. In which growth medium do the seeds germinate first? Which one is most conducive to healthy growth? How does the amount of volcanic ash effect the germination and growth of plants?

3. Take two paraffin blocks (approximately 4" x 6") and cut them into the shape of Earth crust plates. Put them on a hot plate and slowly move them in opposite direction (using heavy-duty gloves) to examine how plates move and react.

4. Invite students to compare the photographs in this book with volcano photos in other books. What similarities are there? What kinds of differences are noted? How can students account for the differences in photos of the same volcanoes? Encourage students to record their ideas in journals.

5. Invite students to create a flip book illustrating the sequence of activities during a volcanic eruption.

6. Encourage students to place the titles of the four different kinds of volcanoes on separate sheets of paper. Invite them to draw illustrations of selected examples (from around the world) of each type of volcano.

7. Invite students to make charts of the dormancy periods of selected volcanoes. For example, which volcanoes have remained dormant the longest? Which volcanoes have had the most recent eruptions? Where are the most dormant volcanoes located? Where are the most active volcanoes located?

8. Invite children to locate information on the "eruption rates" (the length of time from the start of the volcano until it "settles down") for different volcanoes. How can they account for the wide variation in rates?

9. Encourage students to investigate the heights of different active and inactive volcanoes around the world. During a volcanic eruption, how much of the mountain is lost?

10. Invite students to construct comparative charts of volcanoes according to different climatic regions of the world (e.g., How many active volcanoes are located in tropical regions compared with polar regions?). Is there a relationship between climate and the location of volcanoes?

11. The following Web sites were both created by students (a class of third- and fourth-grade students developed the first, and a group of seventh-grade students developed the second). Invite students to log on to these sites and evaluate the information presented. Is it complete? Is it appropriate for the designated grade level(s)? Is any data missing on either site? If students were to create their own Web sites about volcanoes, what type of information would they want to include? Plan sufficient opportunities for students to discuss the elements or features they would want to include on their Web sites.

http://hammer.ne.mediaone.net/earth_force/default.html
http://www.Germantown.k12.il.us/html/volcanoes.html

Chapter 5

Earthquakes

September 1, 1923

Japan is situated directly over a spot on the Earth's surface where two tectonic plates (the Philippine Plate and the Pacific Plate) are moving under a third tectonic plate (the Eurasian Plate); this process is known as subduction and results in high levels of stress and pressure along the fault lines. As a result, Japan is the site of frequent earthquakes—so many, in fact, that tremors are felt every few weeks or so.

The frequency of those tremors did not prepare the people of Japan for one of the most devastating earthquakes in recorded history. On September 1, 1923, the sea floor under Sagami Bay (about 50 miles south of Tokyo) shifted. The ground under the seaport of Yokohama shook for nearly five minutes (the earthquake was later measured at 8.3 on the Richter scale—a massive tremor). More than 300,000 buildings in Yokohama and Tokyo were destroyed, not just by the earthquake, but also by the raging fires spawned by the tremors.

Unbelievably, more than 100,000 people lost their lives in this devastating earthquake. Just as disastrous as the quake and the ensuing fires was a powerful tsunami that swept through coastal villages and towns, virtually clearing the landscape of human habitation. In less than 24 hours, a second powerful quake struck the area, and a series of powerful aftershocks rumbled through the Earth for several days. The Great Kanto Earthquake (as it was to be called) paralyzed the Japanese capital of Tokyo and dozens of surrounding cities for several weeks.

49

The Science of Earthquakes

The Earth's surface is covered by a series of tectonic plates, which are large land masses that "float" on the Earth's mantle—an 1,800-mile thick layer of very heavy, melted rock. As the plates move, they run into or pull away from each other. This produces enormous strains on the rocks near the edges of these plates. Energy builds up along the edges, and one day the rocks suddenly snap past each other. The spot where this occurs is usually the epicenter of an earthquake.

Shock waves emanate from the epicenter of the quake and through the surrounding rocks. These shocks may last for just a few seconds or several minutes. The intensity and duration are what cause so much damage on the Earth's surface. Aftershocks, which are weaker shocks that also release pressure, may follow an earthquake for several days or weeks.

Earthquakes are measured using one of two scales: the Modified Mercalli scale, which measures the intensity of damage, and the better known Richter scale, which measures the magnitude of energy an earthquake releases. Following is a brief description of the Richter scale:

- Magnitude 1–2: Earthquake can only be detected with instruments (more than 500,000 each year).

- Magnitude 2–3: Earthquake can be felt only slightly (more than 100,000 each year).

- Magnitude 3–4: Earthquake can be felt only slightly; little damage (more than 10,000 each year).

- Magnitude 4–5: Earthquake can be felt strongly; windows crack, buildings damaged (more than 1,000 each year).

- Magnitude 5–6: Earthquake can be felt strongly; walls crack (more than 200 each year).

- Magnitude 6–7: Earthquake can be felt severely; buildings collapse (more than 20 each year).

- Magnitude 7–8: Earthquake can be felt severely; ground cracks and buildings collapse (more than 10 each year).

- Magnitude 8–9: Earthquake causes massive damage; buildings collapse, roads buckle (up to 10 each year).

It is important to note that the Richter scale is a logarithmic scale, which means that an earthquake measuring 5.0 is 10 times more severe than one measuring 4.0. An earthquake that measures 7.0 is 100 times more powerful than one measuring 5.0.

Earthquakes

Seymour Simon

New York: Morrow, 1991

Summary

In this visually stunning book, noted science author Seymour Simon presents young readers with an inside look into the science of earthquakes. Youngsters will learn why earthquakes happen, why they occur in certain locations around the world, and what people can do to protect themselves if they experience one of these powerful events. The text is clear and straightforward and the photos are mesmerizing and awe-inspiring. The science of earthquakes, earthquake prediction, and earthquake damage is convincingly presented in the pages of this book. The photos alone will spark conversation and generate a multitude of learning opportunities.

Science Education Standards

The questions and activities in this section can be used to support teaching of the following content standards:

Science As Inquiry

Understanding about scientific inquiry

Physical Science

Properties of objects and materials
Position and motion of objects
Motions and forces
Transfer of energy

Earth and Space Science

Properties of Earth materials
Changes in Earth and sky
Structure of the Earth system

Science and Technology

Understanding about science and technology

Science in Personal and Social Perspectives

Personal health
Changes in environments
Science and technology in local challenges
Natural hazards
Risks and benefits

History and Nature of Science

Science as a human endeavor

Critical Thinking Questions

1. Why do most earthquakes in the United States occur in California?

2. What would be the most dangerous part about an earthquake?

3. How should people prepare for an earthquake?

4. Would you ever consider living in an earthquake-prone area?

5. Would you consider seismology as a career?

6. What would scare you most about an earthquake?

Activities

1. Have students look through the daily newspaper for articles regarding earthquakes. Encourage them to create a bulletin board to display the articles under the heading, "The Changing Earth."

2. Have students create a dictionary booklet titled "My Earthquake Book." Students may wish to create a page for each letter of the alphabet (for example: A = aftershocks; B = boils; C = collapse; D = destruction; E = epicenter).

3. Share one or more videos from the following list. After viewing a selected film, invite students to create a review of the film to be included in an ongoing unit newspaper, *Earth Watch* (specific activities for each film are also suggested).

    This Changing Planet (catalog #30352) available through National Geographical Society, Washington, D.C., explains how the Earth is constantly changing its surface through weather, erosion, earthquakes, and volcanoes. After viewing, invite students to choose one of the ways described in the movie and draw an illustration regarding the event using appropriate captions.

    The Violent Earth (catalog #51234) available through National Geographical Society, Washington, D.C., tours active volcanoes throughout the world. After viewing, encourage students to make a replica of a volcano from modeling clay or papier mâché. Invite students to model their volcanoes after one or more of those in the film.

4. Ask students to maintain an "Earthquake Journal." This can include an ongoing chart of Richter scale readings for the aftershocks that occur in the days and weeks following a major earthquake, photographs or illustrations of the damage observed in various neighborhoods, and lists of earthquake related books located in the local library.

5. Obtain two different colors of modeling clay from a hobby store. Flatten each into a 4-inch square. Place the squares side by side on a smooth surface. Ask one student to place his or her hands on the outer edges of the squares and attempt to push them together.

Encourage other students to note what happens to the clay as it is slowly pushed together. Re-form the squares as above. Repeat the demonstration, asking another student to set the squares side by side. Invite the student to place one hand on one square and another hand on the other and then attempt to move them in opposite directions. Inform students that these two actions are similar to what happens to the Earth's surface during an earthquake.

6. Invite students to log on to the Web site http://www.mindspring.com/~proken. This site provides detailed descriptions and images of earthquakes. It is updated weekly, providing up-to-the-minute information about U.S. earthquakes. Assign various groups of students to record and display the information available on this site for the entire class. A small group of individuals can share important data with the class in a regularly scheduled session during each week of an earthquake study.

7. Have students create an illustration of the different layers of the Earth by painting a huge ball on a piece of poster board. The inside of the ball can be painted in three colors according to the three layers of the Earth (the core, the mantle, and the crust). Students may then wish to use a globe of the world to plot selected countries on their illustrations. They may also wish to plot the locations of some of the major earthquakes that have occurred during the past 25 to 50 years.

8. Encourage students to work in small groups and research other books about earthquakes. Each group may wish to prepare a brief summary on its findings and present its discoveries to the rest of the class. Ask each group to prepare a fact book with the collected data and present their finished products to the school library.

9. Appoint selected students as "Earthquake Monitors." Using one or more Web sites, ask a small group of student to monitor an earthquake that has occurred somewhere in the world. The "team" can issue a daily report to the other members of the class. Reports can be written and posted on a bulletin board or announced, report-style, to the class.

10. Students may be interested in assembling a brochure or newsletter of safety tips for people involved in an earthquake. Divide the class into two groups; one group will prepare a brochure of earthquake safety tips for adults, another will prepare a brochure of safety tips for children. Data for the latter brochure can be obtained from the Web site at http://www.fema.gov/library/quakef.htm. Invite students to discuss any differences or similarities between the two brochures. Where should the brochures be available? How should they be distributed? How can they get into the hands of potential readers before an earthquake strikes?

11. On page 5 of *Earthquakes* (the pages are unnumbered), the author describes fault lines. He presents information on how rocks on one side of a fault push against the rocks on the other side, causing a build up of energy. Over a period of years, friction holds the rocks in place until suddenly, the rocks snap past each other. Students will be able to see this for themselves in the following activity. Provide one student with two wooden blocks (cut off two 6-inch sections from the end of a 2 x 4 piece of wood). Ask the student to wrap one sheet of medium-grade sandpaper all the way around one block and tape it down with masking tape. Repeat for the other block. Ask the student to hold one sandpaper block vertically in each hand. The blocks should be pressed together. While

pressing the blocks together, have the student attempt to slide the blocks in different directions. The two blocks represent the rocks on either side of a fault line. The blocks temporarily lock together (because of the "holding strength" of the granules of sand on the sandpaper). As more pressure is applied to the blocks, the friction between them fails, and they slip past one another. This action is similar to the slippage that sometimes occurs in a fault line.

12.   On the eighth page of *Earthquakes,* the author provides a map of the various earthquake zones in the continental United States. Ask students to post an oversize U.S. map on one wall of the classroom. Have them record on the map the major earthquakes that have struck the United States in the past 100 years. Encourage students to compare the actual locations of major earthquakes with earthquake zones. Have most of the major earthquakes occurred within a "Major" or "Moderate" earthquake zone? Have any earthquakes occurred within a "Minor" or "None" earthquake zone?

13.   After students have completed the activity above, invite them to create a map of the earthquake zones and any major earthquakes that have occurred in Alaska, Hawaii, or both. Which of those two states have experienced earthquake activity? Is there any state that is completely safe from earthquakes?

14.   Invite students to check with the zoning commission in different cities along the West Coast. They may also wish to contact architectural firms, too. Ask students to obtain information on the construction and erection of "earthquake-proof" buildings. What considerations are taken into account during the planning and construction of offices, homes, and shopping malls in areas of the country where earthquakes strike? Students may wish to contact local architects in your town to visit and share information and resources on building codes and requirements in your part of the country in comparison with those in other parts of the country. Provide opportunities for students to share their information with other classes.

I Didn't Know That Quakes Split the Ground Open

Claire Oliver

Brookfield, CT: Copper Beech Books, 1999

Summary

Filled with short, pithy facts and engaging illustrations, this entry in the I Didn't Know That… series provides students with information and engaging data about earthquakes. The author included some legends and myths about earthquakes, information on several "famous" earthquakes in recent years, and various types of rescue efforts used to locate earthquake victims. There are many quizzes sprinkled throughout the text and a great deal of well-defined vocabulary. This book is ideal for independent reading assignments.

Science Education Standards

The questions and activities in this section can be used to support teaching of the following content standards:

Science As Inquiry

Understanding about scientific inquiry

Physical Science

Properties of objects and materials
Position and motion of objects
Motions and forces
Transfer of energy

Earth and Space Science

Properties of Earth materials
Changes in Earth and sky
Structure of the Earth system

Science and Technology

Understanding about science and technology

Science in Personal and Social Perspectives

Personal health
Changes in environments

Science and technology in local challenges
Natural hazards
Risks and benefits

History and Nature of Science

Science as a human endeavor

Critical Thinking Questions

1. Would you want to live in Japan, the most earthquake-prone country in the world?

2. What should young children know about earthquakes?

3. Why are there so many different legends about earthquakes?

4. What is the most dangerous part of an earthquake?

5. Why are aftershocks so dangerous?

6. Why are earthquakes so dangerous in large cities?

Activities

1. Lead students in a guided imagery activity. Encourage them to close their eyes and imagine that they are experiencing an earthquake. Describe the sounds, sights, and sensations that earthquakes cause. Afterward, invite students to create a "graffiti wall" to record personal feelings about the aftermath of that earthquake. Students may post a long sheet of newsprint on one wall of the classroom and invite classmates and others to record their thoughts, feelings, and ideas.

2. Invite students to create a short skit about a make-believe earthquake in their neighborhood. What events happened in the neighborhood? How did the local residents react to those events? Was there a memorable incident that took place?

3. Ask students to create a mock news broadcast about an imaginary earthquake. Selected students can each take on the roles of newscaster, interviewer, local citizens, and interested bystanders to recreate the events that occurred in their neighborhood.

4. Encourage students to work in small groups and research other books about earthquakes (see Appendix A). Each group may wish to prepare a brief summary on their findings and present their discoveries to the rest of the class. Ask each group to prepare a fact book about their collected data and present their finished products to the school library.

5. Invite selected students to work in small groups to construct their own makeshift seismographs. Each group will need a ball of clay, a pencil, a string (approximately 1 foot long), tape, and a white piece of paper. Invite students to tie the string to the eraser end of their pencil and punch the tip of the pencil through a clay ball until just the lead point is sticking out of the clay. Invite one student in each group to tape a sheet of white paper to a desk. One group member can stage an earthquake by shaking the desk

with another group member holding the string up steadily above the desk so that just the tip of the pencil is barely touching the paper. Invite students to observe how their makeshift seismograph records the waves of the "earthquake." Encourage students to compare the recordings they obtained with those found in library books.

6. Provide each of several small groups of students with a shallow pan of water and a marble. Ask individual students to each drop a marble into the pan and describe the ripples that are sent out. Encourage students to compare the waves in their pans with those that might be sent out from the epicenter of an earthquake. Students may also wish to compare their ripples with waves in the ocean. What similarities do they notice? Invite students to record their observations in an appropriate journal.

7. The following Web site provides viewers with eyewitness accounts of the earthquake that took place in Turkey on August 17, 1999: http://turkeyresearch.com/earthquake. Children who lived through the earthquake have provided descriptions of it through photographs, writings, drawings, and paintings, allowing visitors to the site to experience the tragedy of this great earthquake. After students have had an opportunity to view this site, take time to discuss the implications of an earthquake on the lives of children. Do children suffer more in an earthquake? Do children experience more stress? Students may wish to record their thoughts in personal or whole-class journals.

8. Have students write their own newspaper articles about a recent earthquake. Afterward, encourage students to form small groups, discuss their articles, and describe how their work compares with that presented in newspapers or newsmagazines.

9. Ask students to create their own earthquake dictionary. Encourage them to identify one or more vocabulary words for each letter of the alphabet. For assistance, students may wish to log on to http://home.earthlink.net/~torg/eqindex.html. This site is an ABC earthquake site for students, parents, and teachers and includes original, student-created pictures of the terms.

10. Students may be interested in taking a brief quiz to test their knowledge about earthquakes. They can take a 10-question quiz at the following Web site: http://www.worldbook. com/fun/bth/earthquake/html/quakequiz.htm. This quiz might be appropriate for students at the conclusion of an earthquake unit or as a possible extension into a math activity in which students graph and chart their results (or compare their results to those of another class).

11. On page 6 of *I Didn't Know That Quakes Split the Ground Open*, the author describes the longest recorded earthquake in history (Alaska in 1964). Ask students to create a chart of "famous" earthquakes and how long each lasted. Students may wish to research other books listed in this unit, as well as various Web sites. Encourage students to plot these major earthquakes on a map of the world. Where do most of them occur? Is there a pattern of major earthquakes over a particular region of the world?

12. On page 9 of *I Didn't Know That Quakes Split the Ground Open,* there is an easy-to-do activity that illustrates seismic waves. Following is a modification of that activity to help students understand the movement of waves through the Earth. Place four or five similarly sized hand towels (each of a different color) on top of each other (the towels represent the layers of the Earth). Place several toy houses, cars, and buildings (items

from the game Monopoly® would be appropriate) on top of the stacked towels. Invite a student to place one hand at each end of the pile of towels. Ask the student to press down and then to begin pressing the towels together horizontally. Invite other students to note how the towels (the layers) begin to buckle as they are pressed together. (Make sure students understand that this may take hundreds of years to occur in the Earth, even though it is demonstrated in a period of a few minutes with the towels.) Now, ask the student to quickly move her or his hands back to their starting position (a rapid snapping motion may be necessary). Invite students to discuss what happens to the items on the top towel. Students will note that the items shift and several will fall over. This is similar to what happens to structures on the Earth's surface when an earthquake strikes.

13. On pages 12 and 13 of *I Didn't Know That Quakes Split the Ground Open*, the author describes the Mercalli scale for measuring earthquakes (based on what earthquake victims report and the damage sustained by buildings). Included with the descriptions are illustrations of the effects of different levels of earthquakes. Students may wish to take the information presented and create a series of illustrations of local buildings and structures in the surrounding community and the damage they might incur at various levels of earthquakes (according to the Mercalli scale). Students may wish to work in small groups to assemble a gallery of illustrations portraying the damage in the local area if an earthquake were to strike.

14. The book notes that the Northridge earthquake, which occurred in and around Los Angeles in 1994, was the costliest natural disaster in U.S. history. Invite small groups of students (a "hurricane" group, a "tornado" group, a "volcano" group, etc.) to research Web sites on the Internet to discover the costs involved with recent natural disasters. Invite students to construct a chart or graph of the "Top 10" costliest natural disasters in U.S. history. Was the Northridge earthquake the costliest? Which type of natural disaster costs the most each year in the United States?

15. Ask students to do the activity on page 16 of the book. Encourage them to discuss the implications of building structures on wet versus dry sand. Students may wish to relate their observations to descriptions of the damage incurred in San Francisco's Marina District during the 1989 earthquake (as described in *Earthquakes* by Seymour Simon, above).

Shock Waves Through Los Angeles

Carole G. Vogel

Boston: Little, Brown, 1996

Summary

It was one of nature's most astonishing and most devastating events. It occurred without warning or notice, yet it was felt for miles around and for weeks thereafter. It was the Northridge earthquake, which struck Los Angeles in the predawn hours of January 17, 1994, jolting residents of Southern California out of their beds—and their complacency. Highways bridges toppled, water mains ruptured, fires raced throughout neighborhoods, and more than 100,000 buildings were damaged or destroyed. In this mesmerizing book, Carole Vogel offers an eyewitness account of this powerful disaster and the effect it had on the lives of thousands of people. The drama is real, and the events are stunningly depicted in the tragedies and rescues that occurred in every community. This book is both story and science, a fascinating addition to any library or classroom.

Science Education Standards

The questions and activities in this section can be used to support teaching of the following content standards.

Science As Inquiry

Understanding about scientific inquiry

Physical Science

Properties of objects and materials
Position and motion of objects
Motions and forces
Transfer of energy

Earth and Space Science

Properties of Earth materials
Changes in Earth and sky
Structure of the Earth system
Earth's history

Science and Technology

Abilities of technological design
Understanding about science and technology

Science in Personal and Social Perspectives

Personal health
Changes in environments
Types of resources
Science and technology in local challenges
Natural hazards
Risks and benefits
Science and technology in society

History and Nature of Science

Science as a human endeavor

Critical Thinking Questions

1. After reading this book, would you want to live in Los Angeles?

2. Where do you think the long-anticipated "Big One" will strike?

3. What was the most frightening event in this book?

4. What would you like to say to the children whose photos appear in this book?

5. What were some of the effects of the various power failures?

6. If you were a rescue worker, what do you think would be your primary responsibility?

Activities

1. Invite students to share their thoughts and feelings about living through a violent earthquake (such as the one that occurred in Los Angeles). Invite each student to record his or her thoughts in a personal journal. Students may elect to share their thoughts and feelings in small or large group settings.

2. Have students each create a collage (using photos cut out of the newspaper or selected newsmagazines) that replicate the major events of a recent earthquake. Ask students to share their finished products with the class and arrange them into an appropriate display in the classroom (bulletin board, poster, collage, etc.). Students may wish to include appropriate captions for selected photos.

3. Ask students to interview adults in their neighborhood concerning their feelings and emotions about an earthquake. What would they do? How would they feel? How do the emotions they expressed differ from those recorded in students' journals? Students may discuss similarities and differences.

4. Invite students to use play houses and other models to create a make-believe town located on a fault line. Encourage students to assemble a town on a large sheet cake (see "Cakequake! An Earth-Shaking Experience" by Garry Hardy and Marvin Tolman in *Science and Children* Vol. 29 [September 1991], pp. 18–21). Have students make a videotape of the effects of their earthquake.

5. Obtain a free set of curriculum materials from the Federal Emergency Management Agency (FEMA). Write to FEMA (P.O. Box 70274, Washington, DC 20024) on school letterhead. Ask for *Earthquakes: A Teachers Package for K–6 (FEMA 159)*. The organization will provide one free copy per school, while supplies last.

6. When an earthquake strikes somewhere in the world, ask students to write stories about it from different points of view. These might include community impact, human interest stories, geologic impact, and so forth. Students can combine various stories into a special publication.

7. The following Web site can be an excellent source of information, particularly when studying earthquakes in California: http://quake.wr.usgs.gov/recenteqs/. At this site, students can obtain current and recent information about California quakes. Students will see a plot map of the state with ever-changing markers for earthquakes that have occurred in the last hour, day, or week (when recently accessed by the author, this site plotted 231 earthquakes on the California map). You may wish to invite students to report (on a daily basis) the status of earthquakes in California. Students may wish to transfer some of the data on this site to a wall map of California. Invite students to note any trends in earthquake activity around the state. This is one of the most fascinating and interesting Web sites on earthquakes and can be an important part of any earthquake study.

8. If possible, create some color photocopies of the photos in this book (as well as other earthquake books as listed in Appendix A). Invite students to arrange the photos in a horizontal pattern (along one wall of the classroom) according to how scientists might rank them on the Mercalli scale. For example, photos that show little damage might be placed at the left side of the wall, whereas photos showing considerable damage might be placed closer to the right side of the wall. (You may find it helpful to tape a strip of adding machine tape to the wall with Mercalli scale numbers printed on it. The photos can be taped above the strip.) If possible, invite a geologist or seismologist from a local university or college to visit your room to check out the "earthquake wall." How would that individual "rank" the photos along your makeshift Mercalli scale?

9. Using the color photocopies from the activity above, invite small groups of students to create a fictitious story about people or events in a selected photo. The photos and stories can be gathered together into a journal or scrapbook and shared with other classes.

10. An earthquake produces seismic waves that move through the Earth toward its surface. Two types of waves are known as pressure waves and transverse waves. Following is an activity that will help students understand these two wave types. Obtain a toy Slinky® and lay it on a flat table. Invite two children to each hold one end of the Slinky. Ask the students to move their hands back and forth in a coordinated fashion (as one pushes forward the other pulls back). This illustrates a pressure wave, which can move forward and back. Then, invite the two students to wriggle their hands back and forth from left to right horizontally. The Slinky rings now move from the left to the right (or right to left) as undulating waves moving along the length of the Slinky. This movement illustrates a transverse wave that moves either side-to-side or up-and-down through the Earth.

11.   Students may enjoy creating their own "earthquake dictionary." Invite small groups of students to gather selected earthquake terms, vocabulary, concepts, or specific disasters for identified letters of the alphabet. For each of the identified terms, invite students to provide supplementary information, illustrations or photos (as appropriate), Web sites, children's literature selections, or other reference and resource materials that help define specific items. Here are a few examples:

A—aftershock

B—body waves, bridges, buildings

C—crust, core, cracks, California

D—density, damage

E—earthquake, epicenter

12.   Many communities, towns, and cities have individuals employed to enforce building codes. If possible, invite one of these local officials to visit your classroom and discuss building codes in the neighborhood or city. What is a building code? Why are they necessary? Why do some cities have building codes that are different from those in other cities? Would the building codes in effect in the local community be sufficient to prevent extensive building damage in the event of an earthquake? Could the buildings in our town withstand an earthquake similar to the one that struck Los Angeles on January 17, 1994?

13.   If possible, invite one or more rescue workers from the local fire department, police station, or Red Cross agency (depending on your community) to visit your classroom. Before they arrive, provide them with color photocopies of some of the photos from *Shock Waves Through Los Angeles*. Invite the visitors to discuss the rescue efforts depicted in selected photos. What were some of the challenges that rescuers in Los Angeles faced? What were some of the difficulties? The photos on the pages 3, 5 (top), 10, 12 (top), and 18 might be appropriate for this activity.

14.   Encourage students to prepare and present a series of radio announcements about the Northridge earthquake. Invite students to imagine that they are news reporters stationed in various locations around Los Angeles. Each reporter, or team of reporters, can refer to information or photographs in the book to prepare their individual reports. Each team can report their respective observations according to a predetermined time line of breaking events.

Volcanoes & Earthquakes

Eldridge M. Moores

New York: Time/Life Books, 1995

Summary

This is an exciting and dynamic book for intermediate readers. Strong, colorful illustrations permeate every page, providing students with carefully detailed and scientifically accurate explanations of geological forces. A lively text and short, pithy chapters keep interest levels high while developing important concepts and highlighting valuable data. This is both a reference source and an engaging book. Part of The Nature Company's series of books on natural phenomena, students and teachers will turn to this edition many times during a study of earthquakes.

Science Education Standards

The questions and activities in this section can be used to support teaching of the following content standards.

Science As Inquiry

Understanding about scientific inquiry

Physical Science

Properties of objects and materials
Motions and forces
Transfer of energy

Earth and Space Science

Properties of Earth materials
Changes in Earth and sky
Structure of the Earth system
Earth's history

Science and Technology

Abilities of technological design
Understanding about science and technology

Science in Personal and Social Perspectives

Personal health
Changes in environments
Types of resources
Science and technology in local challenges

Natural hazards
Risks and benefits
Science and technology in society

History and Nature of Science

Science as a human endeavor

Critical Thinking Questions

1. What did you learn about earthquakes that you didn't know before?

2. What are some of the similarities between volcanoes and earthquakes?

3. After reading this book, would you want to live in an earthquake-prone area?

4. What is unusual about some buildings in an earthquake-prone area?

5. Why is "liquid soil" a danger in an earthquake?

6. Which is more dangerous, an earthquake or a volcano?

Activities

1. If possible, obtain two or more of the videos listed in Appendix C. Show these films to your students and invite them to discuss the similarities between the events portrayed in the film(s) and those described in the book. Encourage students to create a Venn diagram illustrating the similarities and differences.

2. Ask students to write their own personal newspaper article about a recent earthquake. Afterward, encourage them to form small groups and discuss how their articles compare with the descriptions given in the book.

3. Invite students to construct a model of the different layers of the Earth by painting a huge ball on a piece of poster board. The inside of the ball can be painted in three colors according to the three layers of the Earth: the core, the mantle, and the crust. Afterward, students may wish to use a globe of the world to plot selected countries on their illustrations. They may also wish to plot the locations of some of the major earthquakes that have occurred during the past 25 to 50 years.

4. As a follow-up to the activity above, invite students to log on to the following Web site: http://www.crustal.ucsb.edu/ics/understanding/globe/globe.html. At this site, students will see a rotating globe, which plots earthquakes that have occurred during the past five years. Students also have the opportunity to change the view orientations (Equator, 45 degrees North, 45 degrees South, 90 degrees North [North Pole], and 90 degrees South [South Pole]) to view earthquakes from several different perspectives on the spinning globe. Students also have the capability of pausing the rotating globe or changing its rate of revolution.

5. When an earthquake strikes somewhere in the world, invite students to portray in a mural the events and circumstances that occur. If available, show students examples of Diego Rivera's murals throughout Mexico (check with the school's art teacher). Encourage small groups to create an oversize mural of earthquake events for posting in the hallway, cafeteria, or gymnasium. As additional events unfold, they may add additional illustrations to the mural.

6. Invite a psychologist, counselor, or mental-health professional from a local community agency to come and speak to your class. Ask the individual to discuss the emotional impact that a major natural disaster, such as an earthquake, has on the general population. Who is affected more, children or adults, men or women? Invite students to pose a series of specially prepared questions to the visitor about mental health services available in the local community.

7. Invite students to report on natural disasters that have occurred in their community or geographic area. They may wish to contact the local newspaper for past articles, write to local officials for their recollections, or visit with residents at a senior citizen center. Encourage students to compile their information into a journal or newsletter to share with other classes.

8. Students may wish to log on to the following Web site: http://wwwneic.cr.usgs.gov/ neis/eqlists/10maps_usa.html. On this site, they will find two listings; one records the 15 largest earthquakes in the United States, and the other lists the 15 largest earthquakes in the contiguous United States. For each listing, there is a hyperlink so that students can easily obtain more information and data on a specific earthquake. Invite students to collect data on several earthquakes and to assemble the information into one large journal or notebook. They can donate the notebook to the school library.

9. The following Web site provides a host of interactional, hands-on, and integrated activities for any study of earthquakes: http://www.thetech.org/exhibits.events/online/ quakes/. It also has an introductory section that allows teachers to review the basic concepts of earthquakes, including plate tectonics, waves, seismographs, and other relevant data. Another valuable site is http://geohazards.cr.usgs.gov. This site includes valuable information, as well as an "ask a geologist" page, where students may e-mail earthquake-related questions to scientists.

10. If your classroom computer has a sound card, students may enjoy logging on to this site: http://www.earthshky.com/Kids/Audio/RA/Vol2/Kids16.ram. Here, students can listen to a radio show about earthquakes. After they have listened to the information, invite them to create their own radio call-in show. Other students in the school can be invited to submit earthquake-related questions to your students, who can answer them on the school's intercom system on a regular basis (every Tuesday morning, for example).

11. On pages 16 and 17 of *Volcanoes & Earthquakes,* the author describes several legends and folktales about volcanoes and earthquakes. Students may be interested in researching various Web sites, children's literature, or other resources on differing legends about these natural disasters. Divide the class into several groups and invite them to collect sufficient information on a legend to develop a mini-book or brochure. These booklets can become part of the classroom library.

12. On pages 34 and 39, the author describes different types of instruments and machines used to measure and detect earthquakes. Ask students to create a poster illustrating and describing each of these devises in detail. If possible, invite a local geologist to visit your classroom to describe their function for your students.

13. You may wish to plan some time for students to discuss the similarities and differences between volcanoes and earthquakes. Why did the author decide to include both of these natural disasters in one book? Students can post a large chart comparing these two events along one wall of the classroom.

Chapter 6

Floods and Tsunamis

Summer 1993

The Mississippi River forms an enormous flood plain from Wisconsin south to Louisiana. A slow-flowing river, it carries vast amounts of soil and silt from the riverbanks, earning it the nickname "Big Muddy."

From November 1992 through the summer of 1993, this region of the country received more than 50 inches of rain. Heavy rains continued through the summer, straining the dikes and levees that had been built to contain the river water. Swollen by the heavy rainfall, the river burst open or overflowed from more than two-thirds of the levees. Water inundated farms, towns, and cities, covering more than 17,000 square miles of land. The flooding started on July 4, but it wasn't until August 10 that the waters began to recede and people could begin to rebuild their town, their homes, and their lives. In all, this devastating flood killed more than 50 people and left 70,000 homeless.

The Science of Floods

A flood occurs when a body of water rises and overflows onto normally dry land. Basically, there are two types of flooding: coastal flooding and river flooding. Coastal flooding frequently is caused by high, wind-generated waves and high tides combined with severe storms such as hurricanes. This type of flooding is of special concern because of the large numbers of people who live along the coast in several countries. For example, in 1970, a major storm in the Bay of Bengal produced heavy seas that inundated the coastal regions of East Pakistan, killing some 200,000 people and destroying vast expanses of farmland.

River floods occur when large quantities of water (rain, snowmelt, and ice jams) occur along the length of a river. As a result of continuous and sustained wetting, the ability of the soil to absorb the increased water diminishes rapidly. The longer a rainstorm (for example) lasts, the more likely that rainwater will flow across the ground as runoff and enter stream channels.

Another type of flooding, known as "flash floods," occurs when 10 inches or more of rainwater falls on an area—typically a mountainous area where steep slopes cause water to travel at high speeds—eroding and carrying away debris. These floods are usually short lived, rarely lasting for more than a few hours. Their danger lies in the fact that they occur without warning and can be powerful and highly destructive.

April 1, 1946, and May 22, 1960

On April 1, 1946, shortly after sunrise, a series of giant waves devastated the town of Hilo on the island of Hawaii. Traveling 2,300 miles from the Aleutian Islands in less than five hours, the waves struck without warning and claimed 159 lives. Fourteen years later, on May 22, 1960, a massive earthquake occurred off the coast of Chile. The earthquake generated waves that sped across the Pacific at 442 miles per hour, reaching Hilo in just 15 hours. The first wave to hit the town was a modest 4 feet higher than normal, but the second was 9 feet higher. Before the third wave could arrive, a tidal phenomenon known as a bore smashed into the Hilo waterfront, with 35-foot waves that wrenched buildings off their foundations. That day several city blocks were swept clean of all structures, and 61 people died.

The Science of Tsunamis

Tsunamis often are incorrectly referred to as "tidal waves," although they have nothing to do with the tides, which occur because of the action of the Moon and sun on the ocean. A tsunami (soo-NAH-mee) is a series of waves most commonly caused by a violent movement of the sea floor. When a rock is thrown into the middle of a pond, it sends out a series of ripples. A tsunami is similar—but on a much grander scale.

Tsunamis are generated by one of three different geologic activities. The most usual is a submarine earthquake, when a section of the Earth's crust under the ocean is thrust upward or suddenly drops. The second cause of tsunamis is landslides. A landslide may occur along a section of coastal land or may occur entirely underwater. Volcanic action is the third cause of tsunamis. In these cases, violent volcanic activity near shore or underwater may spawn a series of waves. Of all three types, the most devastating are those caused by large submarine earthquakes.

Tsunami waves are quite different from other ocean waves. Ordinary waves are caused by wind blowing over the surface of the ocean. The water movement in those waves rarely extends below a depth of 500 feet. Tsunamis involve water movement all the way to the sea floor; as a result, the depth of the sea controls their speed. Interestingly, normal ocean waves travel at speeds of less than 60 miles per hour, whereas tsunamis speed across the ocean at an amazing 500 miles per hour.

Most people believe that a tsunami is one giant wave. In reality, they often consist of 10 or more waves that move across the ocean in a "tsunami wave train." Unbelievably, there may be 100 miles separating the wave crests in a wave train. As a result, a tsunami, when it makes landfall, may last for several hours.

Flood

Mary Calhoun

New York: Morrow, 1997

Summary

This is a fictionalized account of one family's struggles during the disastrous Midwestern floods of 1993. Sarajean and her family must make difficult and painful decisions as flood waters inch higher and higher. Sandbags only delay the inevitable as the family comes together for their one and only choice. This is a story of human tragedy, heartache, and misery that accompanies a natural disaster, but this book also celebrates the human spirit and the determination and tenacity of people working together for a common cause. This is a timeless tale to share with listeners of any generation. Its strength lies in the poignant way the author puts a human face on a terrifying event. A great read-aloud book!

Science Education Standards

The questions and activities in this section can be used to support teaching of the following content standards.

Science As Inquiry

Abilities necessary to do scientific inquiry

Physical Science

Motions and forces

Earth and Space Science

Properties of Earth materials
Changes in Earth and sky

Science and Technology

Understanding about science and technology

Science in Personal and Social Perspectives

Personal health
Changes in environment
Science and technology in local challenges
Natural hazards

History and Nature of Science

Science as a human endeavor

Critical Thinking Questions

1. What did you admire most about Sarajean?

2. Is Sarajean's grandmother similar to anyone in your family or any of your friends?

3. What would you find the scariest part of a flood?

4. Why do you think the family felt so strongly about staying in their house?

5. What do you think happened to the house at the end of the story?

6. What would you like to say (if you could) to Sarajean at the end of the story?

Activities

1. Invite students to log on to the Public Broadcasting System Web site org/newshour/ infocus/floods.html to track current information about floods. Here they will learn about floods, flood fighters, and pet rescues, and experience floods through real audio. This is a super site with fascinating information.

2. Ask your students to compose an essay on what they would want to take with them if a flood were approaching their house. Suggest that they can only take those items that they could carry in their arms in a singled trip. What is most important to them? What do they value most? Plan time to discuss students' responses to this assignment.

3. Invite a meteorologist or weather forecaster from the local television station or college to visit your class. Suggest that the individual share information on the causes of floods and why they are so prevalent in certain areas of the country.

4. Have students look through several old magazines and prepare collages of some of the materials (e.g., wheelbarrows, shovels, ladders, etc.) that the people in the book might have used in their fight against the rising waters. Post the collages on a classroom bulletin board for all to see.

5. Encourage students to measure and calculate the amount of water it would take to fill your classroom up to the 5-foot level (for example). They will need to calculate the dimensions of the room (in cubic feet), determine the amount of water (in gallons) of 1 cubic foot, and then multiply the two figures.

6. The author of *Flood* doesn't tell readers what happens after the flood. Invite your students to write a conclusion to the story. What happened to the family? What happened to the house? Plan time to discuss the various endings that students create.

7. Invite students to investigate some of the dangers of building homes on a flood plain. They may wish to start by contacting FEMA (Federal Emergency Management Agency) and their all-inclusive Web site. Some students may wish to contact insurance agencies in town and ask the agents for information on the difficulties of insuring homes and buildings in flood plain areas. Other students may wish to contact one or more environmental groups in your area to inquire about the value of flood plains to the flora and fauna that live in a particular area (along the banks of the Mississippi

River, for example). Hydrologists or structural engineers can be consulted for their views on the hazards of flood plain construction and the special considerations that must be taken into account. Small groups of students may wish to pool their information to create an informative bulletin board display or brochure on the challenges of human habitation in flood plain areas.

8. Ask students to obtain several different water samples from in and around their homes (e.g., tap water, water from a standing puddle, rain water, etc.). Have them place several coffee filters over each of several glass jars and then pour each of the water samples into a separate jar. Ask students to note the impurities that have been "trapped" by each of the filters. Which type of water has the most impurities?

9. The following activity provides youngsters with a chance to see what a raindrop looks like. Invite children to fill cake pans (9 x 15 inches) with about 2 inches of sifted, all-purpose flour. At the start of a rainstorm, encourage kids to stand outside for a few moments and collect approximately 30 to 50 raindrops in the flour (This should be done quickly and at the beginning of a rainstorm; just a few moments in the rain will be sufficient). Have students bring their pans inside. Allow the pans to sit overnight.

   The next day, encourage children to gently sift through the flour and gather up all the congealed raindrops they can. Have them organize the drops on a flat surface (the kitchen counter). They will note that rain drops come in two basic sizes, large and small (large rain drops fall from higher clouds and thus gather more moisture than small raindrops).

   Children may wish to preserve their raindrops. This can be done by spraying or carefully dipping the drops in a commercial varnish. When dry, youngsters will be able to manipulate the drops in a variety of activities.

10. Invite students to check an almanac for the yearly rainfall in your area. They may then locate several cities in the United States and find the normal annual precipitation. Encourage them to compare the rainfall in several cities with your town or city. Plot the information on a large chart. Have students note any similarities or differences.

11. Obtain a copy of *USA Today*. Show students the color weather map on the back of the first section. Ask students to note the various designations used to record weather information. Encourage them to read through the weather section and note the predictions for their area of the country. Students may create a special weather map similar to that in *USA Today*, but specifically tailored for their geographic region (as opposed to the entire United States).

Flood: Wrestling with the Mississippi

Patricia Lauber

Washington, DC: National Geographic Society, 1996

Summary

Simply put, this is a book that will amaze and inform. In her unique style, Patricia Lauber provides young readers with a true inside look into the power, strength, and devastating effects of floods. Her focus is the immense and overwhelming floods up and down the Mississippi River basin during the summer of 1993. In this eloquent and poignant book, Patricia Lauber describes the history of the region, its dependence on the mighty Mississippi, attempts at controlling and channeling the river, and the river's unstoppable destruction. She also describes the challenges of the future—including loss of wetlands and wildlife habitat and the possibility of the river changing its course. This book can be read aloud or individually. However it is read, it illustrates the power and majesty of nature and the futility of humans in trying to legislate or manipulate the forces of nature.

Science Education Standards

The questions and activities in this section can be used to support teaching of the following content standards:

Science As Inquiry

Abilities necessary to do scientific inquiry
Understanding about scientific inquiry

Physical Science

Motions and forces

Earth and Space Science

Changes in Earth and sky

Science and Technology

Understanding about science and technology

Science in Personal and Social Perspectives

Types of resources
Changes in environment
Science and technology in local challenges
Natural hazards

History and Nature of Science

Science as a human endeavor
Nature of science

Critical Thinking Questions

1.   How did this book help you appreciate the power of floods?

2.   What was the most amazing information you learned about floods?

3.   Do you think a flood like that of 1993 could happen again?

4.   What are some ways people can protect themselves from floods?

5.   Will the United States always be subjected to floods?

6.   Which of the photographs did you find most startling?

Activities

1.   The following activity will illustrate how rapidly nutrients are depleted from the soil during a flood. Add ¼ teaspoon of blue tempera paint (dry) to ½ cup of dry dirt and mix thoroughly. Place a coffee filter in a funnel and set it in a large jar. Pour the dirt into the filter. Pour water into the funnel and note the color running into the jar. Keep adding water and note how quickly the color fades (the paint simulates nutrients in the soil; the continuous flow of water simulates the inundation of floodwaters).

2.   The enormous amount of rain that falls before a flood is part of a regular meteorological process known as the water cycle. Students may wish to create their own "home-made" water cycle to see this entire process in action. Here's how they can do it:

Materials

large glass or plastic bowl

small container (a teacup works well)

small weight (two or three quarters, for example)

plastic wrap

rubber bands

water

Directions

a.   Pour about 1 cup of water into the large bowl.

b.   Place the cup in the center of the large bowl (you may need to weight it down so it doesn't float).

c.   Cover the top of the large bowl with a sheet of plastic wrap. Secure it in place with one or more rubber bands.

d.   Place the weight in the center of the plastic wrap so that it causes a slight indentation in the plastic wrap (Figure 6.1).

e.   Place the bowl outside on a sunny day and observe what happens inside.

After the water begins to warm in the sun, it will evaporate. This water vapor condenses on the underside of the plastic wrap, forming small droplets of water. Because of the slope of the plastic wrap, these droplets will roll down the underside of the wrap and drip into the teacup.

This process will continue for some time (depending on the air temperature, the amount of sunlight, and the time of day). What students see inside the large bowl is the same process—on a smaller scale—that occurs in the atmosphere.

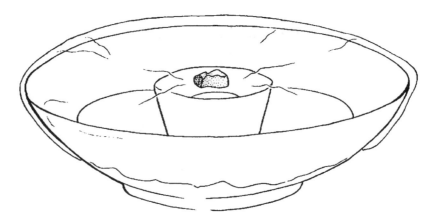

Figure 6.1.

3.   The following activity will help students measure the amount of rain that falls in their part of the world. The instrument they create will help them accumulate rainfall data over an extended period of time (a week, a month, a year).

Materials

tall jar (a tall, narrow olive jar works best)

ruler

felt-tip pen

funnel

Directions

a.   Use a ruler and a felt-tip pen to mark off quarter-inch intervals up the side of the olive jar.

b.   Place a funnel in the jar, then take the jar outside and place in a secure location (the funnel will help collect the rainwater, as well as prevent some evaporation from taking place).

c.   Use a chart or graph and record the amount of rain your area gets in a week or month. Keep an ongoing record.

d.   Students may wish to compare their findings with those reported in the local newspaper.

My Town/City

    One Day _____

    One Week _____

    One Month _____

4.   The Public Broadcasting Service Web site, org/wgbh/nova/flood/, provides students (and their teachers) with up-to-the-minute information about current floods around the country, as well as lesson plans and classroom resources.

5.   Contact the local chapter of the American Red Cross and invite a representative to address your class on the efforts of this organization during a natural disaster, such as a major flood. What are their responsibilities? How can the average citizen become involved in the efforts of the Red Cross during a flood in another part of the country? Students may wish to assemble information into a classroom brochure or notebook.

6.   Invite students to talk about rain and how it makes them feel. They may wish to complete the following sentence stems orally or in writing:

      Rain tastes like_____.

      Rain smells like_____.

      Rain looks like_____.

      Rain sounds like_____.

      Rain feels like_____.

7.   Students may enjoy observing and recording the weather patterns that occur in your area of the country. Be sure students have an opportunity to record weather conditions over a long period of time (2–3 months, if possible). You may wish to create your own "weather notebook" so that students can keep track of rainfall, cloud conditions, temperature, humidity, barometric pressure and so forth. A "Weather Watching Kit" (catalog #5J-738-2253) is available from Delta Education, P.O. Box 950, Hudson, NH 03051. Also available from the company are two classroom weather charts, "Chalkboard Weather Station" (catalog #57-230-1639) and "Weather Chart" (catalog #57-230-1640).

8.   Divide the class into four groups. Assign each group a major flood in U.S. history. Invite each group to create a large, oversized mural of facts for their assigned flood, including illustrations, descriptions, collages, and so forth. Each group can be responsible for adding to its mural for a designated time. Provide opportunities for students to share their murals and to explain why certain objects were placed on the wall.

9.   Invite students to create shoebox dioramas of a flood scene. Divide the class into several small groups. Ask each group to collect various natural objects from around the school or from their respective neighborhoods. Items can include branches, flowers, feathers, dirt, cups of water—anything that may represent the damage or debris that a flood can cause. Invite each group to arrange their collected objects into a three-dimensional display inside a shoebox. Display the dioramas on a ledge or shelf.

10.   Have students create an oversized book (a *big* book) of the Mississippi River Basin, one that includes facts and information about this region of the country. Students can cut the covers into the shape of the basin or the length of the river from two sheets of stiff cardboard and then staple several sheets of paper between the covers. Encourage students to contribute their books to the library.

11.   Ask students to imagine that they are in the middle of rising floodwaters. Encourage them to write a series of imaginary postcards back to their friends. Students may wish to illustrate the front of several blank index cards and write their messages on the back. Completed cards can be posted on a classroom bulletin board.

12.   Have students create an extended time line of significant floods in U.S. history. Post a long sheet of newsprint or an extended strip of adding-machine tape along one wall of the classroom. Invite students to use *Flood: Wrestling with the Mississippi* (as well as other flood-related books) to record significant floods in their proper place on the time line. If appropriate, students may wish to include an illustration of each flood (its location) next to the date of the flood.

13.   If you live near the Mississippi, invite students to plot your location on a map similar to the one on page 8 of *Flood: Wrestling with the Mississippi*. Plan time to discuss the implication of where you live within the Mississippi drainage basin. What can you expect in coming years? How does (and how will) the river influence your lives? Students may wish to make some projections of life in this region of the country in 25, 50, or 100 years. Will the river have changed, or will it change everything around it?

I Didn't Know That Tidal Waves Wash Away Cities

Kate Petty

Brookfield, CT: Copper Beech Books, 1999

Summary

With this book, students will learn some amazing information about wave formation, water movement, tides, and tsunamis. They also will read about various survival stories. Despite the inaccuracy of the book's title, this book provides insightful and compelling information about one of nature's most feared and destructive forces. Ideal as a first look at tsunamis, readers will gain an appreciation for these natural disasters and the ways in which humans have dealt with them throughout history. An abundance of facts and illustrations permeate the pages of this volume, which is particularly well suited for independent research projects.

Science Education Standards

The questions and activities in this section can be used to support teaching of the following content standards.

Science As Inquiry

> Abilities necessary to do scientific inquiry
> Understanding about scientific inquiry

Physical Science

> Position and motion of objects
> Motions and forces
> Transfer of energy

Earth and Space Science

> Structure of the Earth system

Science and Technology

> Abilities of technological design
> Understanding about science and technology

Science in Personal and Social Perspectives

> Changes in environment
> Natural hazards

History and Nature of Science

Nature of science
History of science

Critical Thinking Questions

1.   What is wrong with the title of this book?

2.   Where do most of the world's tsunamis originate?

3.   What are people doing to protect themselves from tsunamis?

4.   How are tsunamis different from regular ocean waves?

5.   How is a tsunami different from a storm surge?

Activities

1.   The following activity will help students understand how waves form.

Materials

9-x-13-inch cake pan

straws

water

blue food coloring

Directions

a.   Place the cake pan on a table and fill it about two-thirds full with water. Tint the water with several drops of food coloring

b.   Hold the straw at about a 45-degree angle and blow across the surface of the water.

c.   Vary the angle of the straw several times and repeat step 2 above.

d.   Vary the force of the "wind" blowing through the straw.

When students blow through the straw across the top of the water, miniature waves are created. As they change the angle of the straw and the power of the "wind" blowing across the water, they also change the size and shape of the ripples or "waves" that move across the miniature ocean.

Winds blowing across the ocean's surface create ripples of waves. The size of a wave depends on the speed of the wind as well as how far the wind has been blowing across the ocean. Large waves form when a steady wind blows great distances across the surface of the sea. Waves can also be formed by undersea events, such as volcanoes and earthquakes.

2.   Waves constantly pound on the shoreline. This is a process that has been going on for millions of years. As a result, rocks are broken down through continual wave action. Following is a fun activity that demonstrates this process.

Materials

white glue

playground sand

water

small coffee can (with lid)

cookie sheet.

Directions

a.   Mix together six tablespoons of white glue with six tablespoons of sand in a bowl.

b.   Using the tablespoon, place small lumps of the mixture on a cookie sheet.

c.   Place the cookie sheet in a slow oven (250 degrees) and "bake" for three to four hours.

d.   Remove the "rocks" and allow them to cool.

e.   Put three or four "rocks" into a coffee can with some water and place the lid securely on top.

f.   Shake for four to five minutes and remove the lid.

The rocks will begin to wear down. Some of the "rocks" will be worn down into sand. The action of the "waves" inside the coffee can causes the "rocks" to wear against each other. As a result, they break down into smaller and smaller pieces. On a beach or shoreline, this process takes many years, but the result is the same. Rocks become smaller as the action of the waves tosses them against each other. Over time, rocks wear down into sand-like particles that eventually become part of the beach or shoreline.

3.   Students may enjoy creating their own tsunami dictionary. Invite them to form small groups, with each group responsible for gathering words and definitions for several letters of the alphabet. For example:

A—Aleutian Islands
    Alaska
B—big waves
C—crest
    Coast Guard
    caldera
D—destruction
E—earthquake
    emergency
    evacuation

       F—fault
       fatal

Students may wish to contribute their class dictionary to the school library.

4. Divide your class into several small groups. Encourage each group to practice reading one of the chapters in the book. Invite the groups to record the entire book on audiotape (several practices may be necessary). Students may wish to suggest several sound effects (e.g., crashing waves, surging surf, etc.). Invite students to contribute the tape to the school library.

5. The author (and editor) of *I Didn't Know That Tidal Waves Wash Away Cities* used an incorrect term in the title of this book because, in reality, a tsunami is not the same as a "tidal wave." *Tsunami* is a Japanese term that translates to "harbor wave." Ask students to discuss why the term harbor wave is a more accurate explanation of these natural disasters than is the term "tidal wave." Provide opportunities for students to discuss their reasons and rationale.

6. *I Didn't Know That Tidal Waves Wash Away Cities* states that the largest tsunami of all time was 295 feet tall. Invite students to locate buildings, structures, or trees in their neighborhood, town, or city that might be close to the height of the highest tsunami. Ask them to imagine a wall of water as high as the highest structure in their town.

7. If possible, obtain a copy of the National Geographic Society video *Killer Wave: Power of the Tsunami* (catalog #51904C; see Appendix C). This film is an excellent introduction to the power and force of these natural disasters. Have students view the video. Afterward, encourage them to compare the information in the book with that presented in the video. What was similar? What was different? Did the video explain any inaccuracies in the book? Do students have any unanswered questions after reading the book and viewing the video? (Note: One of the scientists interviewed on the video is Dr. Walter Dudley of the University of Hawaii at Hilo. Dr. Dudley is one of the world's leading experts on tsunamis and is the director of the Pacific Tsunami Museum; see activity 7 for *Powerful Waves* below).

8. Ask students to imagine that they are having a conversation with Dr. Walter Dudley (see activity 7 above) or another tsunami expert. What kinds of questions would they want to ask? Encourage students to make a list of questions. You may wish to have one student take on the role of a tsunami expert and respond to the questions of other class members. This could be set up like an imaginary news conference with a group of newspaper reporters and the scientific expert.

9. Ask students to blend factual details together in a process known as *word addition*, illustrated with the following examples:

      Underwater earthquake
  + Huge pressure
      ———————————
      Tsunami

In the example above, the phrase *underwater earthquake* was added to the phrase *huge pressure* to create the word *tsunami*. Here is one more example:

Plates pulling apart
+ Magma rising
———————————————
Ocean ridge

Invite students to select some phrases or words from the book and use then to create their own word addition problems. Students may wish to begin by adding two phrases together and progress to the addition of three or four phrases to create unique addends.

10. Ask students to create an ongoing trivia game in which each student contributes 5 to 10 questions and answers. They can play the game regularly (as they accumulate more information about tsunamis) or as a "final exam" at the conclusion of these activities.

11. If possible, invite a sailor or boating enthusiast to your classroom to explain the use of sea charts. Ask the sailor to bring in several charts of a port, a channel, a harbor, a bay, or an ocean. Encourage students to investigate the differences between those charts and land maps. Why are depths indicated on the charts?

Powerful Waves

D. M. Souza

Minneapolis, MN: Carolrhoda Books, 1992

Summary

For thorough, accurate, and compelling information about tsunamis and their power, this book is ideal. The author provides readers with a wealth of information that doesn't overwhelm, but informs and instructs. The author carefully presents information about the formation and definition of tsunamis, as well as their destructive powers, providing readers with scientifically accurate, engaging data that puts tsunamis in their proper context. Highlighted by amazing photos and informative illustrations, this book grabs the reader's attention. This book is an essential addition to any study of natural disasters.

Science Education Standards

The questions and activities in this section can be used to support teaching of the following content standards.

Science As Inquiry

> Abilities necessary to do scientific inquiry
> Understanding about scientific inquiry

Physical Science

> Position and motion of objects
> Motions and forces
> Transfer of energy

Earth and Space Science

> Structure of the Earth system

Science and Technology

> Abilities of technological design
> Understanding about science and technology

Science in Personal and Social Perspectives

> Changes in environment
> Natural hazards

History and Nature of Science

Nature of science
History of science

Critical Thinking Questions

1. Why are tsunamis so unpredictable?

2. What is the greatest danger of a tsunami?

3. Why are tsunamis such a threat to the Hawaiian Islands?

4. Why is the term "tidal wave" inappropriate?

5. What are some ways people can prepare themselves for tsunamis?

Activities

1. Following is an activity that will give students an opportunity to create a homemade "ocean" in a bottle.

Materials

empty 1-liter soda bottle (with a screw-on top)

salad oil

water

blue food coloring

Directions

a. Fill an empty 1-liter soda bottle one-third of the way up with salad oil.

b. Fill the rest of the bottle (to the brim) with water dyed with a few drops of blue food coloring.

c. Put on the top securely and lay the bottle on its side. Now, slowly and gently tip the bottle back and forth. The oil in the bottle will begin to roll and move just like the waves in the ocean. Students will have created a miniature ocean in a bottle.

2. Students can build a three-dimensional model of a shoreline or tidal area with the following activity.

Materials

deep baking pan (a bread loaf pan is ideal)

nonstick vegetable spray (Pam® is a brand name)

4 cups flour

1 cup salt

1½ cups of warm water

acrylic or tempera paints.

Directions

    a.   Knead the flour, salt, and warm water together in a large bowl for about 10 minutes (the mixture should be stiff but pliable).

    b.   Spray the baking pan with vegetable spray.

    c.   Spread the mixture into the pan, forming it into various landforms (beach, rocky shore, sand dunes, outcroppings, cliffs). If necessary, you may want to make more of the mixture using the same recipe.

    d.   Bake in an oven at 325 degrees for about 1 hour or more, depending on size and thickness.

    e.   Test the sculpture for "doneness" by sticking a toothpick into various spots (the sculpture should be firm or hard). If necessary, continue baking the sculpture.

    f.   Remove the sculpture from the oven and allow it to cool.

    g.   Carefully slide the sculpture from the baking pan (an adult should do this part).

    h.   Paint the sculpture with different colors of acrylic or tempera paints (available at art, craft, or hobby stores).

    i.   Optional: When the paint is dry, spray the sculpture with a clear varnish to preserve it.

3.   Underwater, pressure increases by 1 atmosphere for every 33 feet of depth. That means that at sea level, the water pressure is about 14.7 pounds per square inch. At 33 feet below the surface of the ocean, the water pressure is 2 atmospheres, or twice that at sea level (2 x 14.7 = 29.4 pounds per square inch). At 66 feet below sea level, the water pressure is three atmospheres (3 x 14.7 = 44.1 pounds per square inch). This activity demonstrates how water pressure increases with increasing ocean depth.

Materials

    medicine dropper

    tall, deep, clear container (a tall water pitcher)

    water

Directions

    a.   Fill the container with water (select a container made of glass or clear plastic so that students will be able to see through the sides).

    b.   Push the medicine dropper down into the water, open end down, until it reaches the bottom.

    c.   Hold the dropper in this position and invite students to note how some water has entered it.

    d.   Slowly raise the medicine dropper up in the container. As it rises, encourage students to notice how less and less water appears inside the medicine dropper.

Air takes up space, but as the dropper is pushed deeper into the water, the increasing water pressure will compress the air trapped inside the dropper. As it moves deeper into the water, the pressure becomes greater, and more air molecules are compressed ("squished") inside it. As a result, more water can enter the dropper.

In the ocean, water pressure increases at greater depths. At sea level, the water pressure at the surface of the water is 14.7 pounds per square inch. At the bottom of the Mariana Trench, which is 35,827 feet below sea level, the water pressure is 14,622.94 pounds per square inch.

4. Following is a listing of great Web sites on tsunamis, including how they are formed, the destruction they cause, where they occur, simulations and animations, and a host of up-to-date information:

    http://www.Germantown.k12.il.us/html/tsunami.html

    http://www.geophys.Washington.edu/tsunami/welcome.html

    http://www.pmel.noaa.gov/tsunami/

    http://www.usc.edu/dept/tsunamis/

    http://www.thirteen.org/savageseas/Neptune-main.html

    Students can stay up-to-date on the latest events, discoveries, and news about tsunamis by accessing the Web site of the Pacific Tsunami Museum http://www.tsunami.org. Here they can learn about the latest happenings at the museum, contests, and on-going displays. They may wish to gather selected information together in the form of descriptive brochures or pamphlets for the classroom library.

    Students may also wish to write to the Pacific Tsunami Museum to inquire about their educational offerings and displays. The address is: Pacific Tsunami Museum P.O. Box 806 Hilo, Hawaii 96721. (Note: This museum is one of the few tsunami museums in the world. It includes tales of tsunami survivors, the dangers of tsunamis, as well as a variety of tsunami artifacts. The director, Dr. Walt Dudley, is one of the world's leading experts on tsunamis.)

5. Students may wish to observe a miniature tsunami through the following demonstration. Fill a sink up to the rim with water. Take two blocks of wood (cut the ends off a 2-x-4 piece of wood, making each block about 6 inches long) and hold them underwater, one in each hand, so they are slightly below the surface of the water. There should be about 6 inches separating the two blocks. As rapidly as possible, force the two blocks together (end to end). Repeat this action several times. Students will notice that when the two blocks are rapidly compressed together, a swell develops on the surface of the water (water also splashes out of the sink). Because this action is repeated several times, several swells form on the surface. Something similar happens in nature during an underwater earthquake. The ocean floor shifts, rises, or buckles; the ocean water churns; and underwater swells—tsunamis—form.

6. Invite students to log on to the Web site of the Pacific Tsunami Warning Center: http://www.geophys.Washington.edu/tsunami/general/warning/warning.html. Although this site is geared to adult readers, students will be able to learn about the work of this important group and their efforts to save lives and protect property around the world. If

possible, ask students to assemble some of the information on this site into a brochure, newsletter, or pamphlet for other students to read.

7. Students may be interested in a listing of the most frequently asked questions about tsunamis and the work of the International Tsunami Warning System. They can access that information at http://www.geocities.com/CapeCanaveral/Lab/1029/TsunamiFAQ.html.

    After students have viewed the site, ask them to think of any additional questions they may have about tsunamis. Where might they go to discover the answers to those queries?

8. Tsunamis happen most frequently in the Pacific Ocean. Many people believe that they happen almost exclusively in Hawaii or other tropical locations, but tsunamis are a threat and a danger in Alaska as well (there have been six major tsunamis in Alaska since 1899). Students may be interested in learning more about Alaskan tsunamis and how people in that state are preparing for these destructive waves; they can find this information by logging on to the following Web site: http://Vishnu.glg.nau.edu/wsspc/tsunami/AK/AK_waves.html. The Alaska Division of Emergency Services (P.O. Box 5750, Fort Richardson, AK 99505) maintains this site.

9. If possible, obtain a copy of the video *Raging Planet: Tidal Wave* (catalog #51904C; see Appendix C) from the Discovery Channel (unfortunately, they, too, used a misnomer in the title). Have students view the video and focus on the ways in which buildings (particularly those in Hilo, Hawaii) have been constructed so that they can withstand the force of a tsunami. Ask students to check selected buildings in their town or community. How are they different from buildings in a tsunami-prone area? What would have to be done to the local buildings to make them "tsunami proof?" Encourage students to create diagrams or illustrations of the necessary changes.

Chapter 7

Hurricanes

August 24, 1992

It was huge! It was massive! It was scary—really scary! For days, the residents of southern Florida watched anxiously as Hurricane Andrew, the season's largest and most powerful hurricane, took direct aim at one of the country's most populated areas. It was August of 1992. Many Florida residents had been through other hurricanes and had prepared themselves for the inevitable series of hurricanes that typically sweep across the Atlantic Ocean from June to November each year. But they weren't ready for Andrew.

As Andrew approached the Florida coast, it became clear that this was a terrifying storm. Thousands of residents in and around the Miami area packed up their belongings and headed inland for safety. With winds peaking at more than 190 miles per hour, the storm smashed into Florida just slightly south of Miami. The destruction was unbelievable. Houses were ripped from their foundations. Ships and boats were hurled through the air like toys. Whole buildings were torn apart as though they were made of paper. Cars were picked up by the force of the wind and thrown into the ocean.

In all, more than 63,000 homes were destroyed, and 44,000 people were left homeless in Florida and Louisiana. An Air Force base in Homestead, Florida, was decimated. Wild animals from local zoos roamed freely on city streets. Three-hundred-year-old trees were uprooted and tossed about like matchsticks. With more than $30 billion in damage, Hurricane Andrew became this country's most expensive natural disaster in history. It was a storm that would not soon be forgotten, and its scars are still evident today.

The Science of Hurricanes

Hurricanes always form over tropical waters. As the surface of the ocean is heated, moist air begins to rise rapidly. The warm air flows into a low-pressure area, picking up more moisture as it travels. When the warm air rises above the Earth, it cools. The cooling causes moisture to condense into droplets of water that form clouds. As the moisture condenses, it gives off heat, and it is this heat energy that powers the storm. The low-pressure area acts like a vacuum. Warm air is drawn in at the bottom, rises in the column, and spreads out. As the air inside rises and more air is drawn in, the storm grows.

Because the Earth's surface is rotating, the air within the storm travels in a spiral. In the Northern Hemisphere, the spiraling winds travel counterclockwise; in the Southern Hemisphere, they travel clockwise. As high winds develop, air pressure falls rapidly in the center of the storm. This low-pressure area is known as the eye of the storm. The eye may average 14 to 25 miles from side to side in small storms and up to 50 miles across in larger ones.

Hurricanes are large storms that may measure from 200 to 500 miles from edge to edge. A typical hurricane will have sustained winds of 100 to 150 miles per hour; stronger storms might have winds that exceed 200 miles per hour. As it travels over the ocean, a hurricane can pick up as much as two billion tons of water a day through evaporation and sea spray.

Interestingly, most of these storms die out within a few hours; in fact, only about 1 in 10 develops into a full-blown hurricane. In the Caribbean Sea and North Atlantic, these storms are called *hurricanes*; west of the International Date Line, they are known as *typhoons*; and in the Indian Ocean, they are called *cyclones*. The hurricane season in the North Atlantic is from June 1 to November 30. In the Southern Hemisphere, the season is from November to June.

Hurricane

Jonathan London

New York: Lothrop, Lee & Shepard, 1998

Summary

This is a touching and evocative fictional account of a family in Puerto Rico and how they prepare for an oncoming hurricane. Told through the eyes of a young boy, it puts a human face on a natural disaster and its aftermath. The strength of the family is realistically portrayed and wonderfully described in this engaging tale. This book is ideal for reading aloud or as an introduction to any unit on hurricanes. It offers useful insights and a wide variety of curricular extensions in language arts and social studies.

Science Education Standards

The questions and activities in this section can be used to support teaching of the following content standards.

Science As Inquiry

Understanding about scientific inquiry

Earth and Space Science

Changes in Earth and sky

Science in Personal and Social Perspectives

Personal health
Types of resources
Changes in environment
Natural hazards
Risks and benefits

History and Nature of Science

Science as a human endeavor

Critical Thinking Questions

1. What was the most frightening aspect of this story?

2. Why was it important for the family to leave the house?

3.   What might be some of the chores family members will have to do after the hurricane?

4.   Have you ever been in a scary situation with your family? How did you react?

5.   Why was everyone singing in the shelter?

6.   Would your family be prepared to survive a hurricane?

Activities

1.   Students may be interested in obtaining information and relevant facts about hurricanes. The following Web sites provide a wealth of offerings:

   http://www.reedbooks.com.au/rigby/hot/hurrwh1.html

   http://www.macontelegraph.com/special/hurr/hurr.htm

   http://www.jannws.state.ms.us/hrcn.html

   http://www.sun-sentinal.com/storm/history/

   http://www.miamisci.org/hurricane/hurricane0.html

2.   Students may be interested in seeing some real-time videos of hurricanes that have hit the United States in recent years. They can do so at the following Web sites:

   http://rsd.gsfc.nasa.gov/rsd/movies/movies.html

   http://www.discovery.com/stories/science/hurricanes/hurricanes.html

   After students view one or more of these videos, ask them to imagine that they were in the path of one of the storms. Encourage them to discuss some of their feelings about being in such a destructive and violent natural disaster.

3.   Invite students to write a sequel to this story. How can the family best prepare for a future hurricane? What changes or modifications can they make on their home that will help it survive another storm? What kinds of emergency procedures should the family have in place?

4.   Invite a representative of the local chapter of the American Red Cross to visit your classroom. Invite the individual to share emergency preparedness procedures and information about rescue operations that the Red Cross uses in hurricanes. The person may wish to recount the efforts of the Red Cross during a recent storm (hurricane).

5.   Invite students to each create an illustration or collage of a family working together before, during, or after a natural disaster. If desired, students may wish to create an imaginary illustration of their own family during a storm or other catastrophic event. What are the roles and obligations of individual family members during such an event? How would family members work together to survive it?

6.   Following are several Web sites about Puerto Rico that your students may find interesting:

   http://www.house.gov/romero-barcelo/about.htm

   http://www.ocdi.gov/cia/publications/factbook/rq.html

http://welcome.topuertorico.org

http://www.puertoricousa.com

7. After students have had an opportunity to visit one or more of the sites above, invite them to develop appropriate travel brochures for Puerto Rico. Students may wish to organize themselves into small groups and investigate selected aspects of this island territory (geography, government, customs, music, tourist spots, etc.). The class may wish to contact a local travel agency and obtain additional brochures, flyers, and tourist information for inclusions in their own publications.

8. Invite students to gather newspaper and/or magazine articles about weather or to bring in information from daily weather forecasts that are contained in local newspapers or TV news show. Articles can be filed in shoeboxes and shared in a "Weather News" area. Encourage students to examine all of the clippings and compile a list comparing and contrasting the different types of forecasts.

9. Discuss why weather is different from place to place. How can students find out what the weather is like in regions across the United States? What symbols could they use to record and report the weather on a map? Use the map in your local newspaper to find this information. For homework, have students study U.S. weather patterns. Make weather symbols from pieces of construction paper and position them on a map of the United States to denote the weather forecast for a given day. Change these as the conditions change in selected areas.

10. Designate a "weatherperson of the day" to predict the next day's weather. Invite each student to write his or her prediction on a card and put it on the bulletin board to be uncovered the next morning. Be sure to talk about the current weather conditions and how they might effect the weather the following day.

11. When a hurricane is predicted for a specific area of the country (e.g. Gulf Coast, Florida, Eastern Seaboard), have students track the "history" of the storm. They may wish to consult the daily newspaper, a weekly newsmagazine, television or radio broadcasts, or firsthand accounts from meteorologists or weather forecasters. They can collect the "life story" of a hurricane into an album, including a variety of photos and news stories.

12. As a class, students may wish to create a weather dictionary containing all the "hurricane words" they have learned from their investigations. They may wish to complement the definitions with their own illustrations or with pictures from magazines or newspapers.

13. Many local weather forecasters make visits to elementary classrooms as a regular part of their jobs. Contact your local television or radio station to inquire about scheduling a visit from the local weatherperson. Be sure students have an opportunity to generate some potential questions about hurricanes before the visit.

Hurricanes

D. M. Souza

Minneapolis, MN: Carolrhoda Books, 1996

Summary

Using clear text, mind-bending photographs, and lots of maps and diagrams, the author presents a clear and concise explanation of hurricanes. Included in this entry in the Nature in Action series are comprehensible explanations on the formation, power, and destructive capabilities of hurricanes. Readers learn how warmth and water contribute to the generation of a hurricane and how those hurricanes are tracked across the ocean. The author takes readers directly into the eye of the storm where they may learn more about these powerful natural phenomena. The book also includes helpful tips on how to stay safe in a hurricane. This is an engaging and dynamic book for any classroom.

Science Education Standards

The questions and activities in this section can be used to support teaching of the following content standards.

Science As Inquiry

Understanding about scientific inquiry

Physical Science

Motions and forces
Transfer of energy

Earth and Space Science

Changes in Earth and sky

Science in Personal and Social Perspectives

Changes in environments
Science and technology in local challenges
Natural hazards
Risks and benefits

History and Nature of Science

History of science

Critical Thinking Questions

1. What are some of the conditions that create hurricanes?

2. Why do so many hurricanes seem to strike the United States?

3. What is the most dangerous time of the year for hurricanes?

4. Would you ever consider living in a hurricane-prone area?

5. What makes hurricanes so dangerous?

6. What are some ways people protect themselves from hurricanes?

Activities

1. Invite students to log on to the following Web site: http://www.discovery.com/stories/science/hurricanes/create.html. With this site, students can "build" their own hurricane by creating and altering various climatic conditions. They will then be able to track their "homemade" hurricane across the ocean. This is a great site with many interactive possibilities.

2. During the course of a hurricane, numerous trees may be torn from their roots and scattered. Other trees are toppled. Powerful winds affect both large and small trees. The following activity is one way in which students may measure the heights of various trees in their neighborhood. Each child should have two rulers and a length of string. Go outside on a sunny day and locate a nearby tree. Have each student stand a 12-inch ruler on the ground and measure the length of the ruler's shadow. Have each child take a length of string and measure the length of a tree's shadow. Ask children to use the following formula to compute the exact height of the tree:

$$\frac{\text{height of ruler}}{\text{length of ruler's shadow}} \quad X \quad \frac{\text{height of tree}}{\text{length of tree's shadow}}$$

For Example:

Height of ruler = 12"
Length of ruler's shadow = 24"
Length of tree's shadow = 720"

$$\frac{12}{24} \quad X \quad \frac{x}{720}$$

24x = 8640

x = 360 inches (30 feet)
The tree is 30 feet tall.

3. During the hurricane season (June through November), invite students to log on to the following Web site: http://www.gopbi.com/weather/storm/. With this site, students can track the progress of hurricanes in the Atlantic Ocean. This is a great site through

which students can receive hourly and daily hurricane updates, including wind speeds, projected track and actual track, estimated landfall, and a host of other important and valuable information. (Note: This is one of my favorite sites—it's packed with information and provides up-to-the-minute information on any hurricane. It is a great resource for any hurricane study during the fall months).

4. Invite students to create a role-playing situation or simulation. Students can take on the role of local weather forecasters announcing the coming of a hurricane. Have students create a series of weather "broadcasts" over a period of several days. The inclusion of safety tips in these presentations would also be appropriate.

5. Invite students to create a chart similar to the one below. Over the course of the hurricane season, they can record and graph various aspects of all the hurricanes for any respective year.

Name	Location	Highest Wind Speed	Duration

6. Invite students to put together a time line of this country's 10 most disastrous hurricanes. When did they occur? Where did they occur? How much property was destroyed? How many people lost their lives? What were the long-term effects?

7. Divide the class into several cooperative groups. Assign each group a "famous" hurricane from the past. Encourage each group to locate as much information as possible about its hurricane. Each group may wish to post information about their respective hurricane on a specially designed "hurricane bulletin board."

8. Ask students to bring in newspaper accounts of hurricanes during the course of a season. Encourage them to take on the roles of newspaper reporters and develop their own classroom newspaper (*Hurricane Watch*). They can issue the newspaper throughout the school on a daily (or weekly) basis during the hurricane season, keeping students and teachers up to date on the development and progress of selected hurricanes.

9. The following chart lists the number of deaths caused by hurricanes during the decades of the twentieth century. Invite students to create a series of bar graphs that record this information on large sheets of oaktag.

1900–1909....................8,100 deaths

1910–1919....................1,050 deaths

1920–1929....................2,130 deaths

1930–1939....................1,050 deaths

1940–1949....................220 deaths

1950–1959....................750 deaths

1960–1969...................570 deaths

1970–1979...................226 deaths

1980–1989...................161 deaths

1990–1999...................152 deaths

After students have created their charts, invite them to discuss why the number of hurricane-related deaths has declined over the decades of the twentieth century. What factors or conditions may have contributed to that decline? Why were there more deaths in the early part of the century than in the latter part of the century?

10. Before reading *Hurricanes,* invite students to discuss what they would do if a hurricane were to strike their part of the country (if applicable) or if they were caught in a hurricane while on vacation. Ask students to focus on personal emotions (scared, frightened, challenged) and on how a hurricane would impact their families (flooded house, belongings ruined, temporary housing). After reading the book, revisit the earlier conversation and invite students to discuss any change(s) in their perceptions or attitudes about the short- or long-term effects of a hurricane on family life.

11. It is the interaction of low-pressure and high-pressure systems that help create hurricanes. You can help your students appreciate air pressure with the following activity.

Place an old yardstick on a table with about 6 to 8 inches sticking out over the edge of the table. Place a sheet of newspaper over the yardstick and on top of the table. Very quickly strike the end of the yardstick (the part sticking out beyond the edge of the table) with your fist (for safety purposes, make sure students stand back some distance from the table and be sure to wear a set of protective goggles). The stick will probably break or crack (you may wish to practice this activity before demonstrating it for students).

The reason the yardstick broke—even though a single sheet of newspaper covered it—was because of air pressure. Air pressure (at sea level) is about 14.7 pounds per square inch. Thus, there is more than 9,000 pounds of pressure bearing down on a standard sheet of newspaper. Because your fist movement was quite rapid, the air pressure pushing down on the newspaper and stick was greater than the structural strength of the wooden yardstick.

Hurricanes: Earth's Mightiest Storms

Patricia Lauber

New York: Scholastic Press, 1996

Summary

This is a masterful work that examines and effectively describes the power, intensity, and history of hurricanes. Lauber, who conducted thorough research, begins by describing a little-known hurricane that struck the East Coast in 1938. As she tracks the hurricane, readers learn how hurricanes form, how they travel, and the incredible destruction they create across the landscape. In this compelling text, Lauber presents how hurricanes form and how they are named. She also provides information about measuring devices and the scientific tracking of hurricanes, as well as information about the overwhelming destruction they cause. The book ends with an eye to the future and the environmental implications of hurricanes in the years to come. This book is perfect for both independent research and as a classroom read-aloud.

Science Education Standards

The questions and activities in this section can be used to support teaching of the following content standards.

Science As Inquiry

Understanding about scientific inquiry

Physical Science

Motions and forces
Transfer of energy

Life Science

Organisms and environments
Populations and ecosystems

Earth and Space Science

Changes in Earth and sky

Science and Technology

Understanding about science and technology

Science in Personal and Social Perspectives

Changes in environments
Science and technology in local challenges

Natural hazards
Risks and benefits
Science and technology in society

History and Nature of Science

Science as a human endeavor

Critical Thinking Questions

1. Would you want to fly into the eye of a hurricane?

2. What do you think is the most difficult factor in tracking a hurricane?

3. What are some environmental implications of a destructive hurricane?

4. Why do people continue to live in hurricane-prone areas?

5. How far in advance should authorities inform people about an approaching hurricane?

Activities

1. Invite students to imagine that they are in a hurricane-prone area. What types of precautions should they take if a hurricane were approaching? What types of precautions are appropriate at other times of the year? How can families better prepare themselves for future hurricanes? Ask students to assemble a hurricane safety book that they can distribute through a local chapter of the American Red Cross or other disaster relief agency.

2. Invite students to log on to one or more of the following Web sites:

   http://www.discovery.com/stories/science/hurricanes/hurricanes.html
   http://www.macontelegraph.com/special/hurr/hurr.htm
   http://www.discovery.com/stories/science/hurricanes/hurricanes.html
   http://www.worldbook.com/fun/bth/hurricane/html/hurricanes.htm
   http://kids.mtpe.hq.nasa.gov/archive/hurricane/index/html

   After students have looked at several sites, discuss how hurricanes begin, where they occur, and so forth. You may also wish to discuss how hurricane hunters track hurricanes across the open ocean. Have students maintain a weather-report journal throughout the months of September and October using a map of the U.S. Eastern Seaboard (on graph paper). Invite students to track hurricanes as they move across the ocean. With each new hurricane, students can initiate a new log or journal. The results can be transferred to transparencies. Layer the transparencies one on top of the other to compare the various paths hurricanes take across the Atlantic Ocean. As new hurricanes form, invite students to create new transparencies.

3. The *South Florida Sun Sentinel* Web site http://www.sun-sentinel.com/storm/history/ presents students with a time line of the "greatest" hurricanes in history, from the time of Christopher Columbus to the present. Ask students to log on to the site and select the "Top 10" hurricanes of all time. Encourage students to create their own time line of these "Top 10." The time line can be posted on a wall of the classroom.

4. After students have completed the activity above, divide the class into several small groups. Invite each group to discuss the qualities and characteristics that make a hurricane a "great" hurricane. Why are some hurricanes in history better known than others are? Plan time for students to share their impressions about "famous" hurricanes.

5. The book briefly mentions how hurricanes are named. Tell students to imagine that they are in charge of naming the hurricanes for the upcoming hurricane season. What names (in alphabetical order) would they give to the hurricanes? Why are those names appropriate? Inform students that the names used are random and alternate between female and male names. Ask students to consider whether the names should have some sort of historical or personal significance. Encourage students to obtain information on the naming of hurricanes. They may wish to check out the information on page 35 of this book or log on to the various Web sites cited throughout this chapter. Encourage students to construct a chart of names used in the past and names that will be used in the future. How many students in the class have names that have been or will be used to name hurricanes?

6. Invite small groups of students to create graphs or charts of the number of hurricanes that strike the United States for each month of the hurricane season (June to November in the northern Atlantic). The following chart lists the number of hurricanes that struck the United States during the period from 1900 to 1994:

Month	Number of Hurricanes
June	12
July	16
August	40
September	61
October	23
November	6

    Ask students to speculate why September seems to be "hurricane month." What factors or conditions seem to "produce" more hurricanes in September than in any other month? (Students may wish to check information in both *Hurricanes: Earth's Mightiest Storms* and *Hurricanes* by D. M. Souza, described above.)

7. On page 27 of *Hurricanes: Earth's Mightiest Storms*, the author describes the various names given to these storms around the world (e.g., hurricanes, cyclones, typhoons, willy-willies). Invite students to create a poster or mural that describes each of these storms, where they are located, and how they got their names. They can post it on a classroom wall or in the school library.

8. The author describes various meteorological instruments used to measure the weather. If possible, invite a weatherperson from the local television station or a meteorologist from a local college to bring in one or more of the instruments described in the book. Ask the individual to discuss the origin of selected instruments and how they are used to predict weather patterns.

9. The spinning of the Earth (its rotation) effects the way high-pressure and low-pressure masses move. For example, north of the equator air in a high-pressure system turns in a clockwise direction, whereas air in a low-pressure system spins in a counterclockwise direction. Note that this is reversed in the southern hemisphere (high-pressure systems move in a counterclockwise direction, and low-pressure systems spin in a clockwise direction). Because the Earth is spinning faster than the air is moving (known as the "Coriolis Effect"), winds tend to curve in either a clockwise or counterclockwise direction. This can be partially demonstrated with the following activity.

   Very carefully (be sure to wear thick gloves) push a darning needle or wooden skewer through the middle of a ping-pong ball. Hold the needle straight vertically and mark the top of the ball (near where the needle enters) with an "N" for North Pole. Mark the bottom of the ball (near where the needle exits) with an "S" for South Pole. Tell students that this is a model of the Earth (the needle represents the Earth's axis). Twirl the ball from west to east (counterclockwise). Invite students to notice what happens to the "N" (it moves in a counterclockwise direction around the "axis.") . Repeat the counterclockwise twirling motion, but hold the ball above your head. Invite students to notice what happens to the "S" (it moves in a clockwise direction around the "axis.") . This helps explain why hurricanes (low-pressure areas) tend to spin in a counterclockwise motion in the northern hemisphere, whereas typhoons (also low pressure) tend to spin in a clockwise direction in the southern hemisphere.

10. On page 33 of *Hurricanes: Earth's Mightiest Storms* is a map that indicates how four computer programs predicted the path of one hurricane. Invite students to create a similar map for the current hurricane season. Post a large wall map of the United States or the North Atlantic along one wall of the classroom. For each reported hurricane of the season, have students glue a length of colored yarn on to the map (a different color can be used for each hurricane of the season), indicating the path that hurricane takes toward the United States. Plan time at the conclusion of the hurricane season to discuss the different paths various hurricanes took. Students may also wish to create similar maps marking the paths of various hurricanes from past hurricane seasons.

The Magic School Bus Inside a Hurricane

Joanna Cole

New York: Scholastic, 1995

Summary

Here's another entry in The Magic School Bus series. Just like the other books, this one overflows with information and is packed with humor, fun, and an engaging cast of characters. Students will find many tidbits of information and an enormous collection of data to research and discuss. The tone is light, and the facts provide youngsters with an "inside look" at this force of nature. The creation, movement, and destructive power of hurricanes is the focus here. The author also includes an appreciation of the science behind these occurrences.

Science Education Standards

The questions and activities in this section can be used to support teaching of the following content standards.

Science As Inquiry

Understanding about scientific inquiry

Physical Science

Motions and forces

Earth and Space Science

Changes in Earth and sky

Science and Technology

Understanding about science and technology

Science in Personal and Social Perspectives

Personal health
Changes in environment
Science and technology in local challenges
Natural hazards
Risks and benefits
Science and technology in society

History and Nature of Science

Nature of science

Critical Thinking Questions

1. Would you want to be a student in Miss Frizzle's class?

2. How did this book help you appreciate the power of hurricanes?

3. What information do you know about hurricanes that was not included in this book?

4. Which is more dangerous, a hurricane or a tornado?

5. Why do hurricanes cause so much destruction?

6. How should people prepare themselves for hurricanes?

Activities

1. Land absorbs solar energy quickly during the day but loses heat quickly at night. You can help students understand this concept by using two cups of equal size, one filled with soil or sand, the other filled with water. Place a thermometer in each cup and put them in the sun for 30 minutes. Invite students to record the temperatures. Then place the cups in the refrigerator for 5 minutes and read and record the temperatures again. Students should discover that the soil absorbed and lost heat more quickly than did the water.

2. Invite students to log on to the following site: http://www.jannws.state.ms.us/hrcn.html. (This is a complete site where kids can learn all about hurricanes and how to prepare themselves for one.) Based on the information they collect from this site, invite small groups of students to gather important and necessary data on hurricane preparedness that they should share with students in other grades. Should younger students get information different from that given to older students? If so, how should it be different? What is the best type of information to have in the event of a hurricane? Students may wish to create a short video or audiotape specifically designed for kids.

3. Invite students to imagine they are traveling through a hurricane, and then have them write letters or postcards to students in another class describing the experience. Encourage students to describe the adventures they encounter on the journey through the hurricane. You may wish to have students from other classes respond to the missives.

4. Invite your students to write imaginary letters to students their own age who have just gone through a hurricane. What would they want to say? How could they comfort them? What information would your students like to have about surviving a hurricane? If possible, you may want to make prior arrangements with a colleague (who is also teaching a unit on "hurricanes" or "natural disasters") to have her or his students take on the roles of students who have lived through an imaginary hurricane. Those students can reply to your students indicating their current situation and status and how they are coping with the after effects of the hurricane.

5. If possible, obtain a copy of the National Geographic video *After the Hurricane* (catalog #FB58012; see Appendix C). Share this video with your class and then ask them to discuss the after effects of a major hurricane. Invite them to speculate on the effects of a hurricane if it were to strike the area where you live. How would it compare with

those portrayed in the video? What structures, buildings, or other venues in your town or community would the hurricane winds most effect? Students may wish to share their ideas in writing or in an oral format.

6. Invite students to obtain (via the school or public library) one or more of the children's books listed in Appendix A. Encourage small groups of students to create Venn diagrams comparing the information in one of those books with the information presented in *The Magic School Bus Inside a Hurricane*. What similarities do they note? What differences do they discover? Which book has more factual information? Which book is easier to read? Plan time to discuss the comparisons.

7. Students who wish to access up-to-date information about hurricanes and other types of storms can log onto the Web site http://weather.apoke.com/index.html. Here, they will learn how hurricanes form; what a tornado is; and the role of clouds, lightning, and rain in storm formation. Invite students to review the site and note if there is any missing information. After viewing this site, what unanswered questions do they still have? Where can they go to locate the answers to those questions? Here are two other sites students may enjoy:

    http://www.discovery.com/stories/science/hurricanes/hurricanes.html

    http://www.jannws.state.ms.us/hrcn.html

8. On page 17 of *The Magic School Bus Inside a Hurricane,* the author describes the difference between a hurricane watch (a hurricane may strike within 36 hours) and a hurricane warning (a hurricane is likely to strike within the next 24 hours). Plan time to discuss with students the difference between these two terms. Invite students to form two separate lists, one listing the preparations that people should make when a hurricane watch is in effect and those that people should make when a hurricane warning has been issued. Students may obtain the necessary information for these two lists from the Web sites listed above, as well as from relevant children's literature (see Appendix A).

9. On page 24 of *The Magic School Bus Inside a Hurricane,* the author states that lightning can reach a temperature of 50,000 degrees Fahrenheit. On page 26, she states that one thunderstorm can send down 125 million gallons of water in 20 minutes. Share this information with students, and then invite them to create a "world records" book of storm-related facts. What other records (temperature, speeds, rates, amounts) are produced or created during a storm—especially during a hurricane? For example, on page 23, Miss Frizzle states that a typical hurricane lasts for about 10 days. Does that make a hurricane the longest lasting storm in nature? Students may wish to gather their data together into an oversized book to donate to the school library.

10. On page 28 of *The Magic School Bus Inside a Hurricane,* the author includes information on the wind speeds in various parts of a hurricane (e.g., outer hurricane = 40 miles per hour). Invite students to post these speeds on the bulletin board. Encourage them to locate the speeds of other objects (car, train, cheetah, blue whale, etc.) and post their fastest speed on the bulletin board, too. Encourage students to rank order (from low to high) the relative speeds of parts of a hurricane along with other items that may be familiar to students.

11. Invite students to imagine that a hurricane is approaching their local community. What would be some appropriate evacuation routes people could take to escape the damage and destruction? What roads should be used? What roads should be avoided? If possible, obtain a county (or parish) map. Invite students to plot possible escape routes on the map, routes that would allow for the greatest number of people to leave in the shortest amount of time.

12. On page 37 of *The Magic School Bus Inside a Hurricane,* the author describes the difference between a tornado and a hurricane. Students may wish to transfer this information, along with any other information obtained through the Web sites and other children's literature cited throughout this book, into a large Venn diagram posted on the bulletin board. Invite students to decide which storm is most dangerous or most destructive based on their findings.

Stormchaser: Into the Eye of a Hurricane

Keith Elliot Greenberg

Woodbridge, CT: Blackbirch Press, 1998

Summary

This book puts a human face on hurricanes, and especially on the people who track and measure them. The focus is on Brian Taggart, a pilot for the National Oceanic and Atmospheric Administration. Taggart flies into the center of hurricanes with a planeload of scientists and equipment. His job is to pilot the plane into dangerous weather so that meteorologists can plot the force, speed, and direction of these monsters in an effort to save lives and property on land. This is a very interesting book that will open students' eyes to the science of hurricanes and the dangers that scientists must face to gather important information about them. This is an up-close-and-personal profile of a most uncommon person. Eye-catching photos and clear text make this book an important resource for any storm study.

Science Education Standards

The questions and activities in this section can be used to support teaching of the following content standards.

Science As inquiry

Understanding about scientific inquiry

Physical Science

Motions and forces

Earth and Space Science

Changes in Earth and sky

Science and Technology

Understanding about science and technology

Science in Personal and Social Perspectives

Changes in environments
Science and technology in local challenges
Natural hazards
Risks and benefits
Science and technology in society

History and Nature of Science

Science as a human endeavor
Nature of science

Critical Thinking Questions

1.   What do you think is the most dangerous part of Brian Taggart's job?

2.   Would you want to fly with Brian Taggart into a hurricane?

3.   Would you want to have the same job that Brian Taggart has?

4.   Why is Brian Taggart's job so important?

5.   If you could ask Brian Taggart any single question, what would it be?

6.   How do you think the author got the information he needed for this book?

Activities

1.   Invite students to log on to the following Web site: http://www.hurricanehunters. com/askus.htm. At this site, teachers and students can pose questions to the people known as "hurricane hunters"—individuals who fly over and into developing hurricanes. After students are familiar with this site, encourage them to develop a short list of potential questions to pose to the hurricane hunters. What criteria will they use to determine the best questions? For what questions—not answered in *Stormchaser: Into the Eye of a Hurricane* or on the Web site—would they most like answers?

2.   Students may also be interested in logging on to the following Web site: http://www.nhc.noaa.gov. This is the site for the National Hurricane Center, the organization that issues watches, warnings, and forecasts on tropical events in both the Atlantic and eastern Pacific regions. Included on the site are the latest forecasts, storm names, historical storm data, and more. During hurricane season, invite students to track the progression of selected storms across the ocean. They can transfer data from this site to a large wall map for viewing throughout the unit.

3.   Invite one student in your class to take on the role of Brian Taggart. Other students can prepare a set of questions to ask "Brian." Place the fictitious Brian in a chair in front of the class and conduct an interview to learn more about this individual. Here are some modifications of this activity that you may wish to consider:

   a.   The person interviewed is anybody who flies an airplane into hurricanes.

   b.   The person interviewed is a scientist on the ground who monitors hurricanes.

   c.   The interview can be recorded on audiotape for playback as a radio broadcast.

   d.   Conduct the interview over the school's intercom system and invite other classes to contribute possible questions.

   e.   Invite students to prepare a readers theatre script on an interview with Brian Taggart or on the events that might take place during one of his flights.

4. Brian Taggart flies for the National Oceanic and Atmospheric Administration (NOAA). Listed below are several Web sites maintained by this government organization, many of which would be appropriate to use in a series of lessons on hurricanes or a unit on natural disasters:

> NOAA Websites Gallery: http://www.websites.noaa.gov/gallery.html
>
> NOAA Education Web Site: http://www.education.noaa.gov
>
> Developing a Severe Weather Guide for Schools: http://www.nws.noaa.gov/er/ lwx/swep/
>
> Teacher Resource Page: http://www.crh.noaa.gov/abr/teacher/
>
> National Severe Storms Lab Weather Room: http://www.nssl.noaa.gov/edu
>
> Find Your Local Weather Office on the net: http://www.nws.noaa.gov/regions. shtml
>
> Take a daily weather quiz: http://water.dnr.state.sc.us/cgi-bin/sercc/wx-quiz.cgi
>
> Satellite Image of the Day: http://www.osei.noaa.gov/iod.html
>
> NOAA Library and Photo Library: http://www.lib.noaa.gov *and* http://www. photolib.noaa.gov/

5. Ask students to discuss some of the hazards that Mr. Taggart faces whenever he flies his plane into a hurricane. What would be some of the difficulties he would face? How does he prepare for those dangers? Do they think he ever feels scared?

6. Invite students to create an ongoing newscast about one of Brian Taggart's flights. After students have read the book, invite them to create a "you-are-there" newscast as though they were in the airplane with Mr. Taggart and flying into a major hurricane. What events would they report on before, during, and immediately after the flight?

7. On page 11 of *Stormchaser: Into the Eye of a Hurricane* is a chart that describes three types of tropical cyclones. Invite students to develop a large wall chart or poster that displays this information, along with appropriate illustrations (of the storms and their locations) that the class has created. Post this in a prominent place in the classroom.

8. On page 13 of *Stormchaser: Into the Eye of a Hurricane*, the author presents a chart of the Saffir-Simpson Hurricane scale, a system of measuring the strength and intensity of hurricanes. Ask students to create a comparative chart that records the categories and wind speeds of hurricanes with the categories and wind speeds of tornadoes (the Fujita-Pearson Tornado Intensity scale. (Note: This scale can be found in the book *Tornadoes* by Seymour Simon, which is profiled Chapter 8 on tornadoes). Can students draw any conclusions from these two charts? Are there any similarities? What differences do they note? Which storm has the higher wind speeds?

9. On page 24 of *Stormchaser: Into the Eye of a Hurricane*, the author presents a list of hurricane names. Students interested in how hurricanes get their names, in hurricane names that have been "retired," and in a listing of hurricane names (including those for the past several years, those for the current hurricane season, and those for the following hurricane season) should check out the following Web site: http://www.fema.

gov/kids/hunames.htm. Just for fun, students can check to see if their names are on one of the lists.

10. Invite students to contact one or more local environmental groups in your area (addresses can be found in the telephone book) and invite them to share data and information on their group's efforts to clean up the environment after a major hurricane. Students may wish to ask how they and other citizens can become active in the group's efforts.

11. Provide students with a map of the United States and invite them to plot the locations (landfall for the "eye") of the 10 most severe hurricanes in U.S. history. Students may wish to use multiple colors of pencil or chalk to denote the category (according to the Saffir-Simpson scale) of each hurricane. Do they note any trends in the plotted hurricanes?

12. If possible, invite an airline pilot (active or retired) to visit your class and discuss some of the dangers involved in flying into hurricanes. What precautions would she or he take if flying into one of these storms? Would the visitor want to be a "stormchaser" like Brian Taggart?

Chapter 8
Tornadoes

April 1965

It was a calm, peaceful day in the Midwest on Palm Sunday, 1965. People went to church, children played baseball, and families got together to share a day of sunshine and fun. Little did anyone know that this day would be one of the most destructive and deadly in U.S. meteorological history.

It was early in the afternoon when a bank of thunderclouds appeared on the horizon. The storms began to move across Ohio. Soon after, they spawned a deadly series of tornadoes—37 in all. The twisters appeared and disappeared throughout a nine-hour period. They touched down in remote farm fields and in crowded cities, raking the land and causing widespread destruction in many areas of Ohio and in five neighboring states. These tornadoes turned barns upside down. They flung cars through the air as though they were pieces of paper. They leveled houses and flattened shopping centers. They ripped churches from their foundations. They picked up animals and then tossed them across the countryside.

Houses, buildings, and large portions of towns literally vanished. The storm killed 271 people. Such destruction was unbelievable—neighborhoods looked as though an enormous giant had swept them aside; swaths of devastation and death were everywhere. The storm, known as the Palm Sunday Outbreak, was one of havoc, panic, and incredible devastation.

The Science of Tornadoes

Tornadoes are the smallest, most violent, and most short-lived of all storms. They occur almost exclusively in the United States, chiefly in the Mississippi Valley and the eastern half of the Great Plains (Iowa, Kansas, Texas, Oklahoma, Arkansas, Mississippi, Illinois, Indiana, and Missouri). This region of the country often is referred to as "Tornado Alley."

Tornadoes most frequently occur during the spring and early summer, and they usually occur in the afternoon. Tornadoes form when a layer of cold, dry air is pushed over a layer of warm, moist air. (Typically, cold, heavy air moves under warm, light air.) The warm, moist air then quickly forces its way in a spiral movement through the layer of cold air. Strong whirling winds form around a center of low pressure, producing a tornado.

Tornadoes vary in size but can be as much as 1 mile wide. Although a tornado moves in a wandering path at about 25 to 40 miles per hour, the winds within it can spin around like a top and reach speeds of more than 200 miles per hour. Most tornadoes last for approximately eight minutes and travel approximately 15 miles. About 600 to 700 tornadoes are reported in the United States every year.

Tornadoes are classified according to their wind speeds. Meteorologists use the Fujita-Pearson Tornado Intensity scale to rate the intensity of each tornado. The following wind speed classifications are used:

Classification	Wind Speed	Damage
F0	72 MPH	Light
F1	73-112 MPH	Moderate
F2	113-157 MPH	Considerable
F3	158-206 MPH	Severe
F4	207-260 MPH	Devastating
F5	260 MPH	Unbelievable

Eye of the Storm:
Chasing Storms with Warren Faidley

Stephen Kramer

New York: Penguin Putnam Books, 1997

Summary

Warren Faidley is a tornado chaser—he goes wherever the storms are! This is a gripping and amazing look at the life of a storm photographer. Readers get an inside look at the dangers and perils of photographing violent weather, traveling with Warren Faidley as he sets out across enormous distances to record the power and splendor of various weather phenomena. The author describes Warren's life, how and why he chases tornadoes, what he must do to get his photos just right. He also includes information about storm safety. Compelling text is highlighted by some of the most amazing storm photos to be found in any children's book. "Ohs" and "Ahs" will fill the classroom when students get their hands on this volume.

Science Education Standards

The questions and activities in this section can be used to support teaching of the following content standards.

Science As Inquiry

Abilities necessary to do scientific inquiry
Understanding about scientific inquiry

Physical Science

Light, heat, electricity, and magnetism
Motions and forces
Transfer of energy

Earth and Space Science

Changes in Earth and sky

Science in Personal and Social Perspectives

Personal health
Changes in environments
Natural hazards

History and Nature of Science

Science as a human endeavor
Nature of science

Critical Thinking Questions

1.   What do you find most interesting about Warren Faidley's life?

2.   Did the book inspire you to become a storm chaser?

3.   What would you have to know about severe weather to be a good weather photographer?

4.   What kinds of questions would you like to ask Warren Faidley?

5.   Which photograph in the book did you find most interesting?

6.   Why is photographing tornadoes such difficult work?

Activities

1.   Your students may wish to create their own miniature tornadoes with the following activity. Obtain two 2-liter bottles. Fill one bottle approximately two-thirds full with water. Place three or four drops of blue food coloring in the water. If available, sprinkle a little glitter into the water, too. Place the other bottle upside down on top of the water-filled bottle and tape the two bottle tops tightly together. (Note: Many toy stores carry a devise known as a "tornado tube" into which each of the two soda bottles can be screwed to form a complete unit.) Invert the bottles (with the water-filled bottle on top) and, holding both bottles firmly, spin the empty bottle (the one on the bottom) around on its rim in a clockwise motion. The water inside the top bottle will begin to spin clockwise as it descends into the bottom bottle. The shape of that spinning will be similar to a tornado on land. (Note: It may take some practice with the two bottles to duplicate the proper motion.)

2.   Provide opportunities for students to log on to the following Web sites. Each of these sites contains loads of information about tornadoes, survivor stories, data on the Fujita scale, photo galleries, and much more:

> http://tqjunior.thinkquest.org/4232
>
> http://weather.apoke.com/tornadoes.html
>
> http://whyfiles.news.wisc.edu/013tornado/index.html

3.   A class of seventh-grade students created the following Web site: http://www.germantown. k12.il.us/html/tonado.html. Invite your students to log on to it. Afterward, discuss with them the information on the site and how it complements the information in the book.

4.   Invite a local photographer to your classroom. Encourage her or him to talk about the photos in this book and what Warren Faidley had to go through to get the shots he did. What dangers did he face? How complicated were the shots? Could an "average citizen" take photos similar to the ones in the book?

5.   As a follow-up to the activity above, invite one or more local photographers to talk about photography as both a hobby and an occupation. What kind of special training is

necessary? How can one prepare for a career in photography? What education is necessary? How much does the equipment cost? Afterward, students may wish to assemble the information into an informative brochure that they can donate to the school library.

6. Encourage students to develop a list of 10 questions (not answered in the book) that they would like to pose to Mr. Faidley. Where could students go to locate the answers to their questions?

7. Invite students to collect weather maps from the local newspaper for a week. Cut out the maps and arrange them in order on a large sheet of newsprint. Invite students to select a low-pressure area in the western part of the United States and observe how it moves across the country each day. Invite students to check wind directions and their relation to the low-pressure area. Does the low-pressure area result in any severe storms? Do the maps indicate other movements? Where do the fronts and other weather patterns eventually wind up?

8. Plan time to discuss with students the different types of supplies (e.g., to stock a storm shelter) that would be necessary in the event of an advancing storm. Encourage students to compile a list of general supplies such as water, flashlights, blankets, medicines, digging tools. What supplies would be absolutely essential? Students may wish to contact a local emergency relief agency for information.

9. Invite students to talk with the principal about school safety guidelines in the event of a major storm or natural disaster. Is there a plan in place? Are teachers and students adequately informed or prepared? Are there any drills planned for the school year? Encourage students to review the school's or the district's emergency plan and determine its adequacy.

10. Thunderstorms can form when a layer of warm, moist air meets a layer of cold, dry air. A low-pressure area sometimes forms as a result. Students can create their own low-pressure system with the following activity.

    Fill one plastic bucket with very hot water and another plastic bucket with ice water. Obtain an empty (and dry) two-liter plastic soda bottle. Take off the cap and immerse the bottom two-thirds of the bottle into the bucket of hot water (don't allow any water into it). Hold the bottle there for several minutes. Quickly screw the cap on the bottle and immerse the bottom two-thirds of the bottle in the bucket of ice water. Wait for several minutes.

    Students will note that the bottle buckles. This occurs because a low-pressure area was created inside the bottle. The warm moist air inside the bottle produced a small high-pressure area. When the warm air was cooled very rapidly (by being put into the ice cold water), the air pressure was lowered. As a result of the lowered pressure inside the bottle, the sides of the bottle caved in (the air pressure outside the bottle was higher than the pressure inside the bottle).

11. Beginning on page 22 of *Eye of the Storm: Chasing Storms with Warren Faidley,* the author records a Tornado Chase Diary written by Warren Faidley. Invite your students to discuss this section of the book. Afterward, provide individual students with journals or notebooks. Encourage them to record the events and circumstances of an approaching storm in their area. After the storm has passed, provide students with

opportunities to discuss their various observations and emotions about the storm. Were there significant differences in the observations of various students? How would you account for those differences?

12.   As a follow-up to the activity above, encourage students to maintain a Storm Diary during the summer months. Students may wish to e-mail each other to report on their observations and feelings about various storms that pass through your section of the country in the summer. If practical, you may wish to collect these observations and impressions together into a larger journal that can be typed and presented to students at a later time.

The Storm

Marc Harshman

New York: Cobblehill Books, 1995

Summary

This is a touching story about courage in the face of adversity and danger. Young Jonathan hated being different from everyone. He hated being singled out just because he was in a wheelchair. He was happy, though, when he was home with his beloved horses. One day, however, a giant twister roars out of the distance and speeds toward the farm where Jonathan and his family live. Through a courageous act of bravery and daring, Jonathan is able to save his horses. At the end of the tornado's rampage, Jonathan has changed—and so have the people around him. They now see him as an individual, not as just a person with a handicap. This is a wonderful read-aloud story and an engaging accompaniment to any study of tornadoes.

Science Education Standards

The questions and activities in this section can be used to support teaching of the following content standards.

Earth and Space Science

Changes in Earth and sky

Science in Personal and Social Perspectives

Personal health
Changes in environments
Natural hazards

Critical Thinking Questions

1. How is Jonathan similar to, or different from, your friends?

2. What did you admire most about Jonathan?

3. Would you have done what Jonathan did? Why?

4. Is Jonathan someone you would like to have as a friend?

5. Was it brave or stupid of Jonathan to stay in the barn with the horses?

6. Did Jonathan observe proper safety precautions for an approaching tornado?

Activities

1. Discuss why weather is different from place to place. How can we find out what the weather is like throughout the United States? What symbols could we use to record and report the weather on a map? Use the map in your local newspaper to learn this information. For homework, invite students to find out about U.S. weather patterns. Make weather symbols from pieces of construction paper and position them on a map of the United States to denote the weather forecast for that particular day. Change these as the conditions in the selected areas change. As an additional extension, ask students to compare weather conditions in the Midwest with those in your area of the country (If you live in the Midwest, students can compare another area of the country with your specific location.).

2. Designate a "weatherperson of the day" to predict the next day's weather. Invite that student to write his or her prediction on a card and put it on the bulletin board and then uncover it the next morning. Be sure to talk about the current weather conditions and how they might effect the weather the following day.

3. Ask students to write a short poem about their home, their community, or their neighborhood. What are some of the special features and characteristics that the poems should celebrate?

4. Ask students to imagine they are traveling across the Midwest, and have them write letters to students in another class. Encourage each student to describe the adventures encountered on the journey. Encourage students from the other class to respond to those letters.

5. Invite students to collect several copies of travel magazines and brochures about life in the Midwest. Have them prepare a collage of pictures clipped from those periodicals. Plan time to discuss their creations with the entire class.

6. Have students create an imaginary diary titled *A Week in the Life of Jonathan*. Various students can take on the role of Jonathan and record his thoughts and activities over a one-week period. What did he do? What did he see? How did he feel? Students may wish to record Jonathan's experiences from the week just before the tornado or from the week immediately after it.

7. Invite your students to assume the roles of newspaper reporters and to report on the events in *The Storm* as though they were part of the local newspaper. What might be the most significant events that should be included in a newspaper article? Students can each report on different topics, including the tornado itself, the science behind tornadoes, Jonathan as a hero, and the daily challenges of handicapped people.

8. Ask students to write a letter to Jonathan. What would they want to say to him after the tornado? What would they like to ask him? Would they like to meet him? Students may wish to post these letters on the bulletin board.

9. Students may wish to work together to create a large wall mural recounting important scenes from the story. Obtain a large sheet of newsprint from a local hobby store or newspaper office. Using tempera paints, students can work together to illustrate the scenes. Be sure the finished mural is displayed for everyone to enjoy.

10. Have students create a diorama of Jonathan's farm and the surrounding area. Students can create their own three-dimensional objects for the diorama by using the following recipe for simple clay:

Materials

> 3 cups baking soda
>
> 1½ cups cornstarch
>
> 2 cups warm water

Directions

> Pour the baking soda and cornstarch into a medium-sized pot. Add the warm water and mix thoroughly. Heat at a medium temperature until the mixture boils. Stir constantly. Remove the pot from the stove and allow cooling. Add some food coloring (if desired) and knead the clay. It is ready to be shaped into various forms and allowed to dry. Store in a closed container (the clay will dry quickly when left exposed).

11. Invite students to present a mini lesson to another class on tornadoes or "Tornado Alley." The lessons can be presented in person or via videotape.

12. Students may wish to consult such books as *The Old Farmer's Almanac Book of Weather Lore* by Edward F. Dolan (New York: Yankee Books, 1988). Encourage students to create a series of weather maps for different sections of the United States. These maps can be posted throughout the classroom and referred to at various times during a unit on natural disasters. Students may also find the following Web sites useful for this activity:

> http://www.princeton.edu/Webweather/ww.html
>
> http://www.weatheronline.com
>
> http://www.wunderground.com

13. Invite students to check an almanac for the number of storms per year in your area. Then they can locate several cities in the United States (including a few in "Tornado Alley") and find the normal number of storms (or severe weather patterns) for that region. Encourage students to compare the severe weather in selected cities with that of your town or city. They can plot this information on a large chart. Invite students to note significant differences.

Tornadoes

Seymour Simon

New York: William Morrow, 1999

Summary

Mesmerizing photos and crisp, clear text highlight this book about one of nature's most destructive forces. Award-winning author Seymour Simon shares the science behind tornadoes, as well as the human drama behind their fury and power. This book stands out not just as a book about a natural phenomenon, but also as an amazing look into the science of storms. A description of monster tornadoes throughout history and of the strange things that tornadoes do further distinguish this book as a "must have" for any classroom library and any study of natural disasters.

Science Education Standards

The questions and activities in this section can be used to support teaching of the following content standards.

Science As Inquiry

Abilities necessary to do scientific inquiry
Understanding about scientific inquiry

Physical Science

Light, heat, electricity, and magnetism
Motions and forces
Transfer of energy

Earth and Space Science

Changes in Earth and sky

Science in Personal and Social Perspectives

Personal health
Changes in environments
Natural hazards
Science and technology in society

History and Nature of Science

Science as a human endeavor
Nature of science

Critical Thinking Questions

1. What was the most amazing thing you learned from this book?

2. Why should people respect the power of tornadoes?

3. How did the photography in this book contribute to your appreciation of tornadoes?

4. What do you think would be the scariest part about a tornado?

5. What are some ways people can protect themselves from tornadoes?

6. Are tornadoes as powerful as hurricanes?

Activities

1. Invite students to research safety precautions they would have to take during a tornado, at home, school, and after the storm is over. Have groups of two students create tornado safety books to share with their reading buddies (in another grade).

2. Using literature and Web sites, invite students to find out what it is like to be involved in a tornado crisis. Students can interview people who have been involved in tornadoes, read stories, watch videos, do research via the Internet, or correspond with other children who may have experienced a tornado. Students should compile a classroom book or video-recorded weather program or talk show about what it is like to be involved with a tornado, safety precautions that people should take, and the impact these natural disasters have on our communities.

3. Ask students to bring in the Sunday comics. Suggest that they read the comics over the weekend. Model the creation of a tornado comic strip for the class. Divide the students up into groups of three or four. Brainstorm some of the facts that they know about tornadoes that they might wish to include in their informative and amusing comic strip. Invite students to create their own comic strip (pictures and sentences) depicting the development of a tornado and the destruction it can cause. Students can access http://www.chaseday.com and selected literature resources to complete this project.

4. Be a tornado tracker! Pretend that your students are diehard tornado hunters. How would they go about predicting where and when the tornadoes are most likely to roam? What would they pack? What kinds of things would be important to measure while tracking tornadoes? What would they be measuring and why? Some suggested Web sites to provide students with additional information include:

    http://www.wx-fx.com/chase.html. Go into the introduction for the section on storm chasing. This site will provide students with information into the equipment that they may wish to take in their travels.

    http://www.sunnysuffolk.edu/-mandias/honors/student/tornado/intensity.htm. This site provides students with concise details into the grading of tornadoes. Go into the region of measuring tornado intensity. This can be written in a story format if desired.

5. How are tornadoes graded? Invite students to log on to http://www.nssl.noaa. gov/edu/tornado/ and http://www.sunnysuffolk.edu/-mandias/honors/student/tornado/ intensity.htm. How many of each grade of tornadoes were present in the United States during the past three years? Do students notice any patterns? How do students account for these patterns? Go into the area of 1896. Do students have any theories of why 1896 may have been one of the deadliest years for tornadoes in U.S. history? Students may also find the following Web site helpful: http://php.iupui.edu/-eabeaver/toroccur.html.

6. Students may enjoy writing an acrostic poem for tornadoes and accompanying it with an illustration. Display them on a clothesline in the classroom.

    Example

    Thundering clouds loom

    Over our heads.

    Rumbling with an eerie sound,

    Never have I trembled so

    Alas,

    Deadly silence.

    Oh no, we're in the middle of the eye!

7. If you live in a region of the country that is outside "Tornado Alley," you may wish to invite your class to write to students in the region. Log on to http://www.epals.com and set up a pen-pal program between your class and a class in one of the states in "Tornado Alley." Your students may wish to develop a set of questions to ask their pen pals, such as: What is it like living in a part of the country that is prone to tornadoes? What precautions has your family taken? What drills must you practice at school? (Note: If you live in a tornado-prone state, you may wish to establish a pen-pal program with students in another state that is prone to hurricanes, earthquakes, tsunamis, or some other form of natural disaster.)

8. Following are two Web sites that can provide you with important information in designing relevant lesson plans. They are also valuable for older students who would like the most up-to-date information about tornadoes from the scientists who study them.

    The Web site for the National Severe Storms Laboratory in Norman, Oklahoma is http://www.nssl.noaa.gov.

    An all-inclusive site on tornadoes that contains tornado facts, as well as tornado myths is http://www.tornadoproject.com. Tornado media such as books and videos are also available here.

9. Contact the local chapter of the American Red Cross and invite a representative to address your class on the efforts of this organization during a natural disaster such as a tornado. What are their responsibilities? How can the average citizen become involved in the efforts of the Red Cross after a tornado in another part of the country? Students may wish to assemble information into a classroom brochure or notebook.

10.   Invite students to look at selected photographs from *Tornadoes* (the following would be most appropriate: cover, pages 2, 17, 18, and 22; pages are unnumbered). Ask them to describe how they would feel if they were to see one of those tornadoes bearing down on their town or house. What thoughts would be going through their heads? What emotions would they experience? Would they be scared? Plan time in class for students to discuss their feelings and thoughts. If practical, you may wish to invite the school counselor to visit your classroom to talk with students about those feelings.

11.   As a follow-up to the activity above, invite students to look at the photos on pages 9, 10, 14, and 24. Discuss the destruction and devastation portrayed in those photos. How do families cope with such destruction? How would your students cope with that destruction if it were their own house? Besides the destruction of the house, what else does a tornado take away? Again, plan sufficient time for students to discuss and share their feelings and thoughts. You may wish to gather some of those discussions together in a diary or class journal.

12.   The author of *Tornadoes* provides some safety rules and tips that should be followed before a tornado strike. Invite your students to use those rules, along with any others obtained from the various Web sites and literature, to create a brochure of safety tips for students in a lower grade. What should they know? Your students may wish to make a brief presentation to another class on their findings.

Twister

Darleen B. Beard

New York: Farrar, Straus & Giroux, 1999

Summary

Two children, Lucille and Natt, are playing outside when the sky turns an ugly color—a tornado is approaching! They run for the shelter with their mother, but she leaves to help a neighbor, and the two children are left alone to fend for themselves. The twister roars over them, and the children are filled with fear and emotion. Afterward, they push out into the stillness of a desolate landscape and find their mother. This thrilling and exciting story, accompanied by reassuring illustrations, is appropriate for students to read independently at the conclusion of a tornado unit. It captures the fierce beauty of a storm, as well as the strength of a shared experience between siblings.

Science Education Standards

The questions and activities in this section can be used to support teaching of the following content standards.

Earth and Space Science

Objects in the sky
Changes in Earth and sky

Science in Personal and Social Perspectives

Personal health
Changes in environments
Science and technology in local challenges
Natural hazards

Critical Thinking Questions

1. How did the illustrations add to your enjoyment of the story?

2. How would you have felt if you were one of the children in the story?

3. How are Natt and Lucille similar to your brothers or sisters?

4. Why are storm cellars important in various parts of the country?

5. Have you ever been in a scary weather-related event?

6. What would be more frightening, a hurricane or a tornado?

Activities

1. Invite a local meteorologist to visit your classroom to talk about his or her job. Brief your students beforehand so they can generate questions for the guest. Follow up the visit by inviting students to share their thoughts on the topic of being a meteorologist.

2. Invite students to write a prequel or sequel to the story. What could have taken place before the story begins? What will happen after the story? Provide opportunities for students to share their stories with each other.

3. If possible, obtain one of the tornado videos listed in Appendix C. Show the video to your students and invite them to make comparisons between the information in the film and the events of the story. How accurate was the author in portraying the twister in this book? Did the two children do the right thing? What other ways of surviving a tornado are presented in the film?

4. After students have investigated the nature of tornadoes, invite them to write an informational brochure or newsletter specifically for children on what to do in the event of a tornado. What information should they include? How should they write it so that young children will understand it? What should children know about tornadoes so they are prepared in case one strikes when no adults are available to help them?

5. Have students contact one or more emergency agencies (Red Cross, Emergency Preparedness, etc.) in your area (addresses can be found in the telephone book). Invite representatives to share data and information on what they do in the event of a disaster. What services are available for local residents? What educational efforts is the group involved in? Plan time to discuss the emergency preparedness in your area of the country with that which might be available to people who live in "Tornado Alley."

6. Encourage students to conduct some library investigations of the states in "Tornado Alley." What are those states? What are the geographical features of those states? Which of the states experiences the most tornadoes in a year? Which state has had the most destructive tornadoes? You may wish to divide the class into several small groups; each group can be responsible for gathering the necessary information about their "assigned" state and sharing it with the rest of the class.

7. Students may be interested in seeing some photos of tornadoes. The following Web sites offer them a close look at these destructive forces.

    http://www.photolib.noaa.gov/lb_images/nssl/tornado0.htm

    http://tqjunior.advanced.org/4232/photo.htm#7

    After students have seen these sites, provide opportunities for them to share their feelings about the powerful effects of these storms.

8. Provide each of several groups of students with topographical maps of Midwestern states (these can be obtained through your local public library or nearby college). Invite each group to investigate the annual weather patterns for selected areas and the impact of geography on the creation of tornadoes.

9.   Invite selected students to draw a series of illustrations that depict the advancement of a tornado across the prairie. The series of illustrations can be done at 10-minute intervals. Plan time for students to discuss their illustrations with other members of the class.

10. After students have had an opportunity to participate in several of the activities from the "Tornado" section of the book, you may wish to engage them in the writing and production of a readers theatre script, which allows students to incorporate what they have learned into a pleasurable language arts experience. Directions and hints for constructing and using readers theatre in the classroom can be obtained from *Frantic Frogs and Other Frankly Fractured Folktales for Readers Theatre* by Anthony D. Fredericks (Englewood, CO: Teacher Ideas Press, 1993, ISBN: 1-56308-174-1). The following readers theatre script is an example of one you and your students may wish to create for any one of several natural disaster events or circumstances.

The Three Little Pigs in Tornado Alley

Staging

The narrator is at a lectern or podium near the front of the staging area. The three pigs are on stools or chairs. The wolf is standing and moves back and forth between the other characters.

Very Old Pig	Middle-Aged Pig	Very Young Pig
X	X	X

Mean and Grouchy Wolf
X

Narrator
X

Narrator: A long time ago when fairy tales used to be inhabited by animals who could talk and think, there lived these three pigs. Yeah, yeah, yeah. I know what you're saying—each of them built a house, and along came this mean old wolf with incredibly bad breath who blew down the first two houses because they weren't built according to the local zoning laws and then tried to blow down the third house, and he eventually fell into a big pot of boiling water and the three pigs lived happily ever after. Well, that's probably the story you heard when you were a tiny tyke, but that's not the story we're going to tell you today. You see, in this version of the story, the three little pigs decide to move to the Midwest…and you know what happens in the Midwest during the summer months…you do, don't you?

So, anyway, there was this big old farm, and on the farm lived these three brothers who, as you know by now, were pigs. And, as you also know, they were talking pigs. So, one day they were sitting in the living room of their mother's four bedroom condominium going over some of the latest issues of *Better Homes and Gardens*. And that's where our version of the three little pigs begins.

Very Old Pig: Hey, brothers, you know it's about time we moved on out of Mom's house. We're grown up now and ready to go out into the world to seek our fortune. And besides, Mom's getting on in years and won't be able to support us much longer. In fact, pretty soon we're going to have to think about putting her in The Old Porker's Home.

Middle-Aged Pig: You know, brother, you've got a point there. Besides, we wouldn't have much of a story if all we did was sit around Mom's living room discussing the color of her drapes or "500 Uses for Bacon Bits."

Very Young Pig: Yeah! It sure is getting crowded in here, too. You know, since we're pigs, we don't clean up after ourselves, we track mud all over the place, and we make funny grunting noises for most of the day. I think the neighbors are beginning to wonder what we really do. We better move out while we still can.

Narrator: And so it was that the three brothers decided to move out of Mom's house and buy some property in the Midwest. The real estate agent assured them that the land was ideal—rolling hills, lots of space, and no strange animals in the nearby forest.

Mean and Grouchy Wolf: (insulted) Hey, wait a minute! Aren't I supposed to have a place in this story, too?

Narrator: (forcefully) Hey, keep your shirt on! You've been in plenty of stories in the past, so we just decided to give you some small parts in our version of "The Three Little Pigs."

Mean and Grouchy Wolf: Hey, what's going on? Wait until the wolf's union finds out what you guys are doing.

Narrator: Anyway, as I was saying, the three pigs began to build their dream houses along the country road that ran through their property.

Very Young Pig: You know, I think I'll just live in a trailer. They're cheap and easy to take care of, and I can move whenever I want. Besides, how many tornadoes come through this part of the country anyway?

Mean and Grouchy Wolf: Hey, now hold on a minute here! Now, I may not have all the best lines in this story, and I may be the meanest thing on four legs, but I just don't get it. Don't you know that a trailer can be one of the most dangerous places to be during a tornado? It won't give you much protection, and it can easily be picked up and destroyed by even an F0 tornado.

Narrator: Wow! Mr. Wolf sure does know a lot about tornadoes.

Mean and Grouchy Wolf: You bet I do, buster. They can be pretty scary events.

Narrator: Okay, just settle down! Don't have a coronary! Let's just see what happens in the next part of the story. It's all yours, Middle-Aged Pig.

Middle-Aged Pig: Thanks. While you guys were talking, I was just walking around my property gathering some lumber. I think that I'll build my house out of this stuff. It should be pretty sturdy, and it won't fall down the first time I slam the front door.

Mean and Grouchy Wolf: Now just a gosh darn minute here! You want me to believe that this walking pile of pork chops is really going to build a house of wood way out here on the prairie? I mean, isn't he gonna consider any type of protection in case one of those tornadoes decides to roar through here some summer afternoon?

Narrator: Boy, you sure do get pushy. You know, this is supposed to be a story about the three little pigs, not about some wolf with an attitude problem.

Mean and Grouchy Wolf: Look, wise guy, how'd you like me to nibble on your face? And listen up, this is the Great Midwest—you know, "Tornado Alley." I'm just concerned about the safety of my fellow actors, that's all. Don't get in a panic!

Narrator: (indignant) Now, just hold on. We still have to see what Very Old Pig does with his part of the story.

Very Old Pig: You know, they don't call me Very Old Pig for nothin'. In fact, I'm the guy they call on to bring home the bacon…get it? Bring home the bacon! So, while this hot-shot wolf might be trying to huff and puff his way around the country, I'm going to go my brothers one better—I'm going to build myself a storm shelter. I'm going to make it out of bricks and steel and reinforced cement. Ain't nobody going to blow this baby down! I mean this beauty is built! And, I'm going to stock it with some tools and make sure the door is reinforced, That way, if some tornado comes through here, me and my family will have a safe place to stay.

Mean and Grouchy Wolf: Hey, that's pretty smart. You must have read some books on tornadoes and done some tornado activities when you were in school.

Very Old Pig: That's right, bacon breath. My teacher *(teacher's name)* told us about the dangers of tornadoes and ways in which we could protect ourselves from these fierce storms. I mean, that was a long time ago, when I was just a little tyke, but I still remember those lessons today.

Mean and Grouchy Wolf: Wow! And all this time I thought that pigs were just stupid creatures who spent the whole day wallowing around in the mud and grunting for their dinner.

Very Old Pig: Well, guess what, dragon breath—we're actually smarter than you think. In fact, I'm so smart that I'm going to help my brothers build their own storm shelters so that they can have some protection if a tornado roars through here some day.

Mean and Grouchy Wolf: Hey, you ARE some smart pig.

Narrator: So, the three little pigs each built a storm shelter. And, they each got a battery-operated radio to listen for any storm warnings during the annual tornado season where they lived. And, of course, they all lived happily ever after. But, of course, that kind of story would never make for an exciting story for the kiddies. So a long time ago a bunch of fairy-tale writers got together and decided to spice up the story a bit and turn the wolf into a door-to-door salesman with an asthma problem. The rest, as they say, is history. But, of course, you know the really true story of the three little pigs in "Tornado Alley."

Adapted from Anthony D. Fredericks, *Frantic Frogs and Other Frankly Fractured Folktales for Readers Theatre* (Englewood, CO: Teacher Ideas Press, 1993).

Chapter 9

Avalanches and Landslides

January 23, 1998

In was a bright day in Gap, France. Gap is a ski resort high in the French Alps near the Italian border. It is a favorite place for many people who enjoy skiing and hiking through unspoiled mountainous areas. Since the beginning of the week, more than three feet of new snow had fallen in the Alps. The new snow raised the risk of an avalanche, and hikers and skiers were warned to stay on clearly marked trails and paths.

Thirty-four students ranging in age from 14 to 16 and six adult chaperones were on a high school trip. Each strapped on a pair of snowshoes and set off for a day of hiking along the mountainside above the ski station. For some unknown reason, the group strayed off the trail. Several skiers above the group reportedly touched off a massive avalanche—an avalanche that occurred without warning.

A wall of heavy, unstable snow plummeted down the mountainside. The entire group of hikers was swept up in the power and fury of the racing wave of snow. Some who were fortunate enough to be caught at the edges of the avalanche were spared serious injury. Others were not so lucky. As a result, eleven people, including nine students and two adults were killed. Nine others (seven students and two adults) were severely injured and had to be airlifted out by helicopters. The French media called it the country's worst avalanche in a decade.

The Science of Avalanches

Avalanches are significant and dangerous mountain hazards. In the United States alone, they are responsible for more deaths each year than earthquakes. In the western United States, about 100,000 avalanches occur annually and effect some 300 people. Most of the people swept up by avalanches are skiers, snowboarders, or snowmobilers, who typically have gone into areas where they do not belong. There is a mistaken belief that skiers can outrace avalanches. Unfortunately, the truth is that an avalanche can reach a speed of up to 200 miles per hour—nearly five times faster than the fastest skier can move.

Simply defined, an avalanche is a mass of snow moving down a slope. An avalanche may develop during a heavy snowstorm (typically within 24 hours of a snowfall), but most often they occur after the snow has accumulated at a given site over a period of time. During the course of the winter, different storms create different types and amounts of snow. After snow falls, it can change into distinct types of crystal that are affected by temperature and exposure to the sun.

As the season progresses, the snowpack becomes a multilayered "history" of storms and weather. Some layers are strong (the snow crystals bond tightly together), whereas other layers are weak (the snow crystals do not bond tightly). Even deeply buried layers can change because of temperature fluctuations and the weight of successive layers on top of older layers.

The depth of a weak layer of snow determines how dangerous an avalanche will be. Weak layers near the surface produce loose avalanches that are more like sand rolling down a hill. These avalanches are often called *sluffs*. It is when one or more weak layers are buried more deeply that an avalanche becomes dangerous. Typically, these major avalanches are triggered by a stress—a skier or snowmobiler, new or windblown snow, or an explosive. These major avalanches—often called slab avalanches—are large, involve vast quantities of snow, and are unstoppable. Survival in a major avalanche is often a matter of luck—being in the right place at the right time.

November 1985

The town of Amero, once with a population of nearly 30,000 people, is situated in the Lagunella River valley in the heart of Colombia. On a fateful day in November 1985, Nevado del Ruiz, a volcano more than 30 miles away, erupted. The intense heat from that eruption melted the ice and snow at the peak of the mountain, forming a devastating mudflow (known as a "lahar"). These rivers of mud, more powerful than any major river, can cause considerable damage over a widespread area.

Picking up rocks, boulders, and tree trunks the Nevado del Ruiz lahar surged down the valley at breakneck speed. In the middle of the night and without warning, it engulfed the town of Amero in a terrifying 130-foot wall of mud and ash. More than 23,000 people were killed—most in their sleep. Less than 3,000 people survived one of the most devastating mudslides in modern history. Amazingly, however, survivors were found, partially encased in the concrete-like mud, three weeks after the eruption.

The Science of Landslides

Most people don't realize it, but landslides are one of nature's most powerful and destructive forces. Even though landslides are not as spectacular as hurricanes, floods, or earthquakes, they are more widespread and may cause more property loss than any other geologic hazard. Worldwide, thousands of people die every year from landslides and mudslides. In the past 20 years alone, more than 20,000 people have perished in landslides. In the United States, landslides and mudslides cause an estimated $1 to 2 billion in damage and kill 25 to 50 people every year.

Landslides occur when a portion of a hillside becomes too weak to support its own weight. This weakness generally occurs when rainfall or some other source of water increases the water content of the slope, reducing the strength of the materials. If the hillside is dry, dirt and rocks can tumble down the grade. If the slope is saturated with water, a mudslide occurs.

Landslides are typically classified into one of three types. These include *slides*, which move downward as large bodies. This slippage usually occurs along one or more failure surfaces. One of the most expensive landslides in U.S. history occurred in Thistle, Utah, in 1983. The slide, one-half mile from top to bottom, had a width that ranged from 1,000 feet to nearly 1 mile. The damage from this landslide exceeded $500 million.

Another type of landslide is a *fall*. Falls of rock or soil originate on cliffs or steep slopes. In 1903, a mass of approximately 30 million cubic feet of earth and rock fell from the top of Turtle Mountain in Alberta, Canada. This mass spread out over a 2-mile-wide valley, completely eradicating a single town and killing 70 people.

Mudslides or mudflows (also known as lahars) are another type of landslide. These destructive flows are landslides that behave like fluids. As they slip down a slope or mountainside, they can pick up rocks, trees, houses, and cars. Their power increases as they move along – gathering momentum and increasing their strength. They often reach speeds of up to 60 miles per hour. They bury buildings and sweep away homes. Nothing can stop them.

Avalanche

Stephen Kramer

Minneapolis, MN: Carolrhoda Books, 1992

Summary

This is a book that will enthrall and excite students. Overflowing with dynamic and awe-inspiring photographs and crisp, sharp illustrations, this book effectively brings into focus the dangers of these natural disasters. Stephen Kramer offers readers an inside look at avalanches and provides information and data that everyone who lives or travels in snow country needs to know. Kramer not only covers basic topics such as where avalanches occur, types of avalanches, and rescue techniques, he also presents necessary facts about how avalanches are controlled and the fundamentals of avalanche safety. There is much to discover and learn in this intriguing book.

Science Education Standards

The questions and activities in this section can be used to support teaching of the following content standards.

Science As Inquiry

Understanding about scientific inquiry.

Physical Science

Position and motion of objects
Properties and changes of properties in matter
Motions and forces
Transfer of energy

Earth and Space Science

Properties of Earth materials
Changes in Earth and sky

Science and Technology

Understanding about science and technology

Science in Personal and Social Perspectives

Personal health
Changes in environments
Science and technology in local challenges
Natural hazards
Risks and benefits

History and Nature of Science

Science as a human endeavor
Nature of science

Critical Thinking Questions

1.   Why are avalanches so dangerous?

2.   How should people protect themselves from avalanches?

3.   Why do avalanches happen so often?

4.   Why are trees important in an avalanche?

5.   What makes snow unstable?

6.   What are some of the warning signs of avalanches?

Activities

1.   Invite students to log on to the following Web site: http://www.discovery.com/exp/ avalanche/build.html. With this site, they can build their own avalanche. By manipulating various factors such as a mountain's angle of slope, an increase or decrease in snow depth, the addition or deletion of trees, and a change in the weight of a skier crossing the mountain, viewers can simulate avalanche conditions without going outside. This is an excellent "hands-on" site that effectively demonstrates the factors necessary for an avalanche to occur.

2.   On page 11 of *Avalanche*, the author presents a map of the countries with the greatest avalanche danger. After students have reviewed this map, invite them to post a world map on the bulletin board or one wall of the classroom. Encourage students to identify and label the major mountain ranges in the identified countries. Students may also wish to indicate the various elevations of those ranges as well as their total area.

3.   On pages 16 to 21 of *Avalanche*, the author presents information on the two basic types of avalanches. Invite class members to construct a Venn diagram that outlines the similarities and differences between these two avalanche types. Students may wish to include words, phrases, pictures, or illustration in their diagram(s).

4.   Students can keep up to date on avalanche advisories in Montana through the following Web site: http://www.mtavalanche.com/. They can access information about avalanche warnings and advisories in Colorado through this Web site: http://www. caic.state.co.us/. They can also get up-to-date reports on avalanches on Washington and northern Oregon at this site: http://www.nwac.noaa.gov/nw01000.htm. Ask students to maintain a bulletin board display through the winter months on the avalanche information and advisories in these four states. What similarities do they note? Why would these sites be important for people skiing or snowboarding in Montana, Colorado, Washington, or Oregon?

5. Ask students to log on the following Web site: http://nsidc.org/NSIDC/EDUCATION/ SNOW/web_resources.html. Here, they can obtain the facts and information about snow, a glossary of snow terminology from A to Z, frequently asked questions about snow, and a series of snow crystal images. Invite students to compare the data on this site with that in the book. How has their perception of snow changed as a result of reading the book and obtaining the information from this site?

6. *Avalanche* includes many exciting and dynamic photos of avalanches and the destruction they cause. Students may be interested in how one photographer goes about photographing avalanches. The following Web site offers some incredible data on the steps taken to photograph an avalanche: http://www.pbs.org/wgbh/nova/avalanche/ capture.html. If possible, invite a local photographer in to the classroom to describe the dangers, hazards, or challenges an avalanche photographer would face in gathering necessary shots (those on the Web site or those in the book).

7. On page 20 of *Avalanche*, the author mentions that a slab avalanche travels at about 40 to 100 miles per hour. Invite students to create a chart that lists the top speeds of different forms of transportation (bicycle, skates, running, family car, airplane, train, motorcycle). Encourage students to record the top speeds from low to high. Where does the speed of an avalanche fall on that chart? Is the speed of an avalanche faster or slower than humans can run? Is an avalanche speed faster or slower than the family car? Plan time to talk with students on why it is virtually impossible to outrace an approaching avalanche.

8. If possible, obtain photographs of any mountains in your general area or region of the country. If you live in a relatively flat area, obtain photographs of mountains from other parts of the country. Make several color copies of those mountains. Provide each of several groups with a collection of color copies. Invite students to review the information about avalanche paths on pages 27 to 29 of *Avalanche*. Then, encourage each group to imagine that the mountains in their photos are covered with snow. Ask students to use markers or pens to draw in a starting zone, one or more tracks, and one or more runout zones for an imaginary avalanche that might occur on each mountain. Plan time for students to share their illustrations and note any similarities. Students may wish to post these on a special bulletin board for all to see.

9. The author presents information on preventing avalanches and guiding avalanches. Ask students to create two wall charts using those titles. Encourage them to brainstorm for additional ideas that could be included on each chart, ideas that go above and beyond the ones mentioned in the book. For example, the author suggests that trees and snow fences can be used to prevent an avalanche. What other devises—natural or manufactured—could be used to prevent potential avalanches. Walls, snow rakes, and snow sheds are used to guide avalanches down a mountainside. What other artificial means can students suggest for this specific chart?

10. Here's a Web site that can become an important adjunct to any avalanche study: http://www.avalanche.org. Students will find a page that not only lists all the North American Avalanche Centers in Canada and the United States, but has hyperlinks to each of those centers as well. Students can get up-to-the-minute information on the status of avalanches in a particular area and learn about each center's efforts to

inform the public. After students have viewed the site, divide the class into several groups. Assign one of the centers to each group and invite each group to make brief reports (orally or in writing) on a periodic basis about the ongoing efforts of the assigned centers.

11.   The author includes a chapter on avalanche safety. After students have read that chapter invite them to log on to the following Web site: http://www.mountainzone.com/features/avalanche. Here, they will find additional information on avalanche safety. Invite students to compare and contrast the two sources and encourage them to discuss which source is most complete, most up-to-date, and most helpful—particularly for people who do not normally live in parts of the country that experience avalanches.

12.   For students who want more in-depth information about avalanches they may wish to log on to: http://www.avalanche.org/~1safc/TUTORIAL/TUTORIAL.HTM. This site has just about anything one might wish to know about avalanches. Included are hyperlinks to frequently asked questions, avalanche education, avalanche publications and videos, avalanche glossaries, snow and avalanche graduate-degree programs, the Natural Disaster Database Search Engine, snow research and snow crystal links, as well as many other avalanche-related Web sites. There's plenty to search and plenty to learn at many of these informative sites.

Landslides, Slumps, and Creep

Peter Goodwin

New York: Watts, 1997

Summary

This is a fascinating book about a little-known and little-understood natural disaster—landslides. Few people realize that, worldwide, landslides cause billions of dollars in damage and thousands of deaths and injuries each year. The author provides readers with pertinent information about landslides (the movement of a large mass of dirt and rock over nonmoving material), slumps (a landslide over a curved surface), and creep (a slow-moving landslide with no observed line between moving and nonmoving parts). The author presents convincing and fascinating evidence, including the fact that most parts of the country are subject to landslides (some more than others), and offers necessary prevention measures that people should follow. This book is an exciting read filled with tons of information and loads of eye-popping photographs. It's sure to generate much discussion.

Science Education Standards

The questions and activities in this section can be used to support teaching of the following content standards.

Science As Inquiry

Understanding about scientific inquiry

Physical Science

Position and motion of objects
Motions and forces

Earth and Space Science

Changes in Earth and sky

Science in Personal and Social Perspectives

Personal health
Changes in environment
Natural hazards
Risks and benefits

Critical Thinking Questions

1. Why are landslides so dangerous?

2. Why are landslides considered natural disasters?

3. Is it possible for a landslide, slump, or creep to occur where you live?

4. What are some ways people can protect themselves from landslides?

5. Why are landslides often unpredictable?

Activities

1. Invite students to log on to the following Web site: http://www.fema.gov/library/lanslif. htm. This site provides the warning signs for a landslide. Encourage students to print out those signs or to record them on a separate sheet of paper. Ask individual students (or small teams) to visit several different places in the local community. Are any of the signs of a landslide present in the local area? Do windows or doors stick? Are there new cracks in wall plaster? Are there widening cracks in streets or sidewalks? Students may wish to mark any of the signs of a landslide on a map of the local community.

2. After students have viewed the Web site listed above, encourage them to look around their house for ways to minimize a potential landslide. These may include, but are not limited to, planting ground cover on sloping land, building channels or deflecting walls, or redirecting any potential water flows. Encourage students to discuss these plans with their parents or guardians. Small teams of students may wish to assemble an informational brochure on ways families can landscape their property to eliminate any threat of landslides.

3. Students may be interested in viewing photographs of various landslides. They can do so at the following Web site: http://www.ngdc.noaa.gov/cgi-bin/seg/m2h?seg/haz_ volume3.men. Invite them to construct an oversized Venn diagram that compares the pictures on the Web site with those in the book. What similarities do they note? Do all landslides look the same? Do they all behave the same?

4. The following Web site offers students a view of the mudflow that occurred during the 1980 eruption of Mount St. Helens: http://www.pbs.org/wnaet/savageearth/volcanoes/ html/sb1-vid.html. Invite students to view this site and to read the book *Volcano: The Eruption and Healing of Mount St. Helens* by Patricia Lauber, which was profiled in this book in Chapter 4. Invite students to discuss the various natural disasters (earthquake, volcano, landslide) that occurred during that eruption. Encourage students to create a three-part Venn diagram that outlines the effects of these three occurrences on the mountain. How did each natural disaster contribute to the mountain's current condition? What was the effect of the mudflow on the ecology of the surrounding area of Mount St. Helens?

5. As a follow-up to the activity above, invite students to log on to http://www.disasterrelief. org/Disasters/971008landslide. This site offers valuable information and important data about mudslides. After students have had an opportunity to review the site, divide the class into several small groups. Encourage each group to put together an informational brochure on the causes and prevention of mudslides. Students may wish to gear their brochures to an adult or student audience. For comparison purposes, students may

wish to view a student-created Web site on slope failures: http://www.Germantown. k12.il.us/html/slope_failures.html. This site was produced by seventh-grade students and can offer your students additional information for inclusion on their brochures.

6. Students who are interested in "real time" monitoring of an active landslide in California may wish to log on to the following Web site: http//vulcan.wr.usgs.gov/Projects/ CalifLandslide/framework.html. Here, students can get "real-time" data and current landslide information on a specific landslide. Although some of the information is technical, students will be able to see how geologists approach the study of these frequently misunderstood natural disasters.

7. The American Red Cross has assembled a vast amount of important information about landslide awareness, disaster safety information, what to do during a landslide hazard, and resources available after a landslide. The material on their Web site (http:// www.redcross.org/disaster/safety/guide/landslide.html) is thorough, complete, and detailed. After students have had an opportunity to review various sections of this site, invite them to rewrite portions of the text so that it might be useful for younger citizens. Students may wish to work in small groups to prepare a series of informational brochures or distinctive bulletin boards to share data with members of their peer group. What prevention or rescue information would be most useful for students? Additional safety guidelines can be accessed on the following sites: http://walrus.wr.usgs.gov/elnino/ lanslide-guidelines.html and http://www.disastercenter.com/guide/landslide.html.

8. The following Web sites contain a wide variety of photographs of landslides from around the world:

    http://www.dgtl.dpe.go.id/geotek/ba-info-el.html

    http://www.kingston.ac.uk/~ce_s011/landslid/slides.htm

    http://volcanoes.usgs.gov/Hazards/What/Landslides/SlideExamples.html

    Ask students to access one or more of these sites. What similarities do they note in the photographs and slides? Do landslides share any common characteristics? Encourage students to compare and contrast the photographs on these sites with those in the book. Additionally, students may wish to download some of the photos on these sites and use them to create an informative bulletin board display on landslides.

9. In Chapter 4 of *Landslides, Slumps, and Creep*, the author describes several famous and not-so-famous landslides from throughout history and from around the world. Invite students to review these descriptions. Based on the data they have learned from the book, as well as from various Web sites (see above), ask students to create their own landslide-rating guide (you may wish to review the rating systems used for hurricanes, earthquakes, and tornadoes). What kind of numerical guide can they develop that would rate the power, intensity, destructiveness, loss of human life, and property damage of a landslide. Invite several student teams to propose one or more rating systems. Afterward, students may wish to rate a landslide described in the book, as well as those on the Web sites above. Selected landslides can be rank ordered, described, and posted on an appropriate bulletin board.

10. If possible, invite a geologist or Earth science professor from a local college to visit your classroom. Ask the visitor to explain the science of avalanches to your students or comment on the information presented in the book. Depending on where you teach, the geologist may be able to describe nearby areas that might be prone to landslides.

11. Students may wish to create a three-part bulletin board on the three types of landslides: landslides, creep, and slumps. Photos, descriptions, fatalities, financial cost, and property damage may be some of the data that they can record in each section of the bulletin board. Information obtained from interviews with a visiting geologist (see above) may also be included.

12. If possible, obtain a copy of the video *Landslide: Gravity Kills* (catalog #164178; see Appendix C) from the Discovery Channel. Invite students to compare and contrast the information and scenes in the film with those in the book. What information did they find most compelling or awe inspiring?

13. Invite students to collect several copies of travel magazines and brochures from parents or local travel agencies. Based on the information they have learned in this book, invite students to study photographs in the travel literature to determine any mountainous areas that may be prone to landslides. Students may wish to compare specific locations in the travel literature with those profiled in the Web sites listed above. Students may wish to create collages of pictures that feature landslide-prone regions of the world.

Chapter 10

Storms

November 13, 1970

November 13, 1970, may be recorded as the date of the worst storm in history. It happened in the small country of Bangladesh, which is situated at the confluence of three major rivers: the Ganges, the Meghna, and the Brahmaputra. As a result, much of the country is composed of low-lying delta land that is open to the sea and to storms that rage in off the ocean.

On that fateful date in November, one of the most powerful cyclones of all times ravaged Bangladesh. Fierce winds swept over the countryside at speeds of nearly 200 miles per hour, blowing away crudely constructed houses and buildings, which were never to be seen again. The storm carried cattle out to sea and completely obliterated 25 island communities. Enormous tracts of land were swept clean and then inundated with tons of debris that was scattered across the countryside.

The entire delta was transformed. Old rivers and streams were re-formed, and new rivers were created. Floodwaters covered everything, and thousands of corpses—both animal and human—floated in the muck and mud. Crops were ruined, and vast numbers of people began to die from starvation and disease. Estimates vary, but the final figures indicate that between 300,000 and 1 million people died in this all-consuming storm.

The Science of Storms

Storms happen all the time—all over the world. In fact, more than 16 million storms occur every day. Some are short, some are violent, and some leave lasting impressions on the landscape and the memories of those who survive them. A storm can be defined as an atmospheric activity that releases a large amount of energy. A storm may cover a large geographical region or a small local area. Storms may include hurricanes, cyclones, tornadoes, or monsoons. One of the most common and most frequent storms is a thunderstorm.

Thunderstorms are formed when warm, moist air is pushed rapidly upward, accompanied by equally rapid downdrafts of cool air. Lightning, thunder, heavy rain, and strong gusts of wind usually accompany thunderstorms. Most thunderstorms are short, rarely lasting more than two hours, but it is possible to have many thunderstorms in a day.

Thunderstorms are the most powerful electrical storms in the atmosphere. In 20 minutes, a single thunderstorm can drop 125 million gallons of rain and give off more electrical energy than a large city uses in a week. Each year, there are about 16 million thunderstorms around the world.

Basically, there are two types of thunderstorms: air-mass thunderstorms and frontal thunderstorms. An air-mass thunderstorm, often called a summer thunderstorm, is formed within an air mass during hot summer afternoons. It happens when hot, moist air above the Earth's surface rises, forming cumulus, and then cumulonimbus clouds. Most summer thunderstorms are localized. A frontal thunderstorm is formed when a cold front arrives, pushing warmer air ahead of it. This air movement forms a series or long line of thunderstorms, which may be hundreds of miles long and up to 50 miles wide.

Lightning is an electrical discharge within a thunderstorm. During the development of a thunderstorm, the clouds become charged with electricity—up to 100 million volts. Lightning occurs when the voltage in a thunderstorm becomes high enough to speed through the air from one place to another. Although scientists aren't exactly sure why this happens, we do know that a bolt of lightning can reach a temperature of 50,000 degrees Fahrenheit. Obviously, lightning can be extremely dangerous. Every day someone is struck by lightning and injured or killed (a park ranger in Virginia was struck by lightning seven times between 1942 and 1977).

The Big Storm

Bruce Hiscock

New York: Atheneum, 1993

Summary

On March 31, 1982, an enormous storm battered the coast of California with high winds and driving rain. Moving inland over the course of the next six days, it spawned avalanches in the Sierra Nevada Mountains, blizzards in the Rocky Mountains, tornadoes in the Midwest, snow in the Great Lakes, hail in the south, and a foot of snow along the Atlantic seaboard. This book follows the path of that storm, effectively weaving science and geography to illustrate a wide variety of weather phenomena and their effects on humans. Delightful illustrations and compelling text engage young readers. This book should be a staple in any classroom and in any unit on weather studies.

Science Education Standards

The questions and activities in this section can be used to support teaching of the following content standards.

Science As Inquiry

Abilities necessary to do scientific inquiry
Understanding about scientific inquiry

Physical Science

Position and motion of objects
Light, heat, electricity, and magnetism
Motions and forces
Transfer of energy

Earth and Space Science

Changes in Earth and sky

Science and Technology

Understanding about science and technology

Science in Personal and Social Perspectives

Changes in environments
Natural hazards
Risks and benefits

History and Nature of Science

Science as a human endeavor
Nature of science

Critical Thinking Questions

1. What did you find most amazing about this six-day storm?

2. What did scientists learn as a result of this storm?

3. How did the illustrations contribute to your understanding of this storm?

4. If you could ask the author one question, what would it be?

5. Why is the work of meteorologists so important?

6. What was the most amazing storm you have ever experienced?

Activities

1. Invite students to create their own homemade weather station. The following instruments will help them learn about the weather and some of the ways in which meteorologists measure various aspects of the weather.

    a. **Thermometer:** Use a nail to dig out a hole through the center of a small cork. Fill a bottle to the brim with colored water and push the cork into the neck of the bottle. Push a straw into the hole in the center of the cork (see Figure 10.1). Mark the line to which the water rises in the straw with a felt-tip pen. Note the temperature on a regular thermometer and mark that on a narrow strip of paper glued next to the straw. Take measurements through several days, noting the temperature on a regular thermometer and marking that at the spot where the water rises in the straw on the strip of paper. After several readings, students will have a fairly accurate thermometer. (Liquids expand when heated, so water rises in the straw; liquids contract when cooled, so water lowers in the straw).

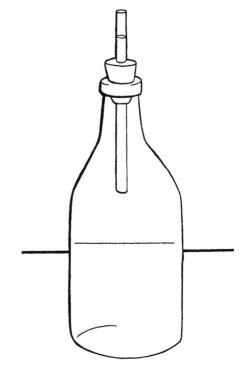

Figure 10.1. Thermometer

b. **Barometer:** Stretch a balloon over the top of a wide-mouth jar and secure it with a rubber band. Glue a straw horizontally on top of the stretched balloon, starting from the center of the balloon (the straw should extend beyond the edge of the jar). Attach a pin to the end of the straw. Place another straw in a spool and attach an index card to the end. Place this device next to the jar so that the pin is close and points to the index card (see Figure 10.2). When air pressure increases, the pressure inside the bottle is less than that of the outside air. Therefore, the balloon rubber pushes down, and the pointer end of the straw moves up; that spot can be marked on the index card. When the air pressure goes down, the air inside the jar presses harder than the outside air. The rubber pushes up and tightens, and the pointer moves down. (Point out to children that when the pointer moves down, bad weather is probably on the way because air pressure falls when a storm is approaching. When the pointer rises, it's usually a sign that good weather is on the way.)

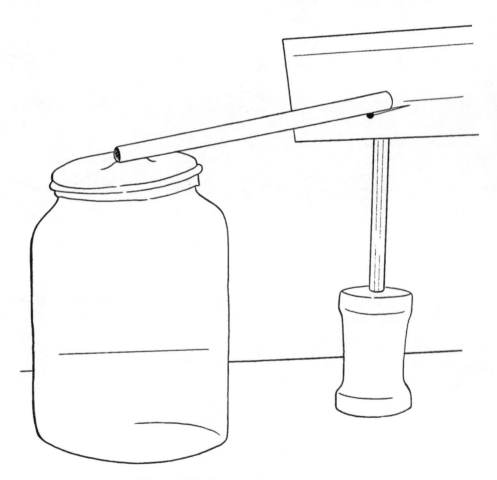

Figure 10.2. Barometer

c. **Anemometer:** Cut out two strips of cardboard approximately 2 x 16 inches. Make a horizontal slit halfway through the strip in the middle of each one so that they fit together to make an "X." Cut four small paper cups so that they are all about 1 inch high. Staple the bottom of each cup to one "arm" of the "X." Use a felt-tipped marker to color one of the cups. Make a hole in the center of the "X" with a needle.

Stick the eye of a needle into the eraser of a pencil and place the pencil into a spool (jam some paper around the sides of the spool hole so that the pencil stays erect). Glue the spool to a large block of wood. Place the "X" on the tip of the needle so that it twirls around freely (see Figure 10.3). Blow on the cups to make sure they spin around freely (some adjustments on the size of the hole may need to be made). Invite youngsters to place their anemometer outside on a breezy day and count the number of times the colored cup spins past a certain point. That will give them a rough idea of wind speed. (Meteorologists use a device similar to this one, but the revolutions are counted electronically.) Later, you may wish to introduce youngsters to the Beaufort scale, a widely used measure to judge the speed of wind.

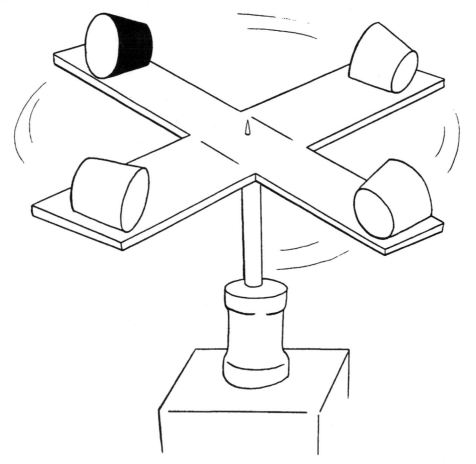

Figure 10.3. Anemometer

Students may wish to set up their makeshift weather station outside and take regular "readings." They can match these measurements with those reported in the daily newspaper. Make comparisons between the students' readings and those from the newspaper. Students should record their readings over a period of several days or weeks in a journal.

2.   Students may enjoy observing and recording the weather patterns that occur in their area of the country. Be sure students have an opportunity to record weather conditions over a long period of time (two to three months, if possible). You may wish to create your own weather notebook so that students can keep track of rainfall, cloud conditions, temperature, humidity, barometric pressure, and so forth. A "Weather Watching

Kit" (catalog #J-738-2253) is available from Delta Education (P.O. Box 950, Hudson, NH 03051). Also available from the same company are two classroom weather charts: "Chalkboard Weather Station" (catalog #57-230-1639) and "Weather Chart" (catalog #57-230-1640).

3. Ask each student to imagine that he or she is a particular form of weather (a raindrop, a gust of wind, a snowflake, etc.). Encourage students to write about their "life cycle" from the perspective of that form of weather. What do they observe? What distances do they travel? How long is their life span?

4. Obtain a copy of *USA Today*. Show students the color weather map on the back of the first section. Have students note the various designations used to record weather information. Encourage students to read through the weather section and note the predictions for their area of the country. Have them compare these predictions with those in the local newspaper. Which is more accurate? Invite students to create a special weather map similar to that in *USA Today*, but specifically tailored for their geographic region (as opposed to the entire United States).

5. Invite students to watch a local television weather report each evening. Encourage them to record the predictions for the weather each day. Then on the following days, invite them to record the actual weather. Discuss with them any differences or similarities between the predictions and the actual daily weather. Invite students to graph and chart their information. How accurate (over an extended period of time) are the forecasters in predicting weather?

6. If possible, invite selected students to take photographs of various cloud patterns. After the photos are developed, ask students to arrange them into an attractive display for the entire class, classifying them into cloud types. Students may wish to include descriptions of each cloud type and what it means in terms of impending weather.

7. Students may be interested in logging on to the following Web site: http://tqjunior. advanced.org/5818/. This site, titled "Weather Gone Wild," offers students an inside look into various types of storms and natural disasters. These include thunderstorms, tornadoes, hurricanes, tsunamis, and avalanches. Also included are weather maps and a glossary. This is an excellent all-inclusive site through which students can obtain a wide variety of important information.

    You may wish to assign several student teams one of the sections of this Web site. Invite each team to gather the necessary information for an informative brochure to distribute to other students at your grade level or throughout the school.

8. What's the rainiest place in the United States? Would it surprise you to learn that it's in Alaska? In fact, three of the five rainiest spots in the United States are all located in Alaska. Here are the figures:

Place	Normal Annual Precipitation
Yakutat, Alaska	134.96 inches
Hilo, Hawaii	128.15 inches
Annette, Alaska	115.47 inches
Quillayute, Washington	104.50 inches
Kodiak, Alaska	74.24 inches

Ask students to collect information from local newspapers, Web sites, or other sources on the annual rainfall in selected areas of your state. Which part of the state is the rainiest? Which part of the state is the driest? Invite students to record their findings on a wall map of your state. If desired, students may wish to create charts that compare the annual rainfall in your state with that of another state.

9. Some scientists estimate that there are about 2,000 thunderstorms in progress over the Earth's surface at any given moment. There are about 45,000 thunderstorms each day and approximately 16 million each year around the world. In the United States, there are at least 100,000 thunderstorms every year. Invite students to create a chart or graph that records those statistics on a daily, weekly, or monthly basis. That is, how many thunderstorms occur in the United States each week (on average)? How many thunderstorms are taking place over the Earth in a month? Students may wish to establish a series of bar graphs that illustrate these numbers.

10. Students may be interested in learning about the training and education required to become a meteorologist. They can find out at the following Web site: http://outreach.ocs.ou.edu/students/careerhelp/. After students have seen the site, ask them to create a brochure or flyer on the educational requirement for a degree in meteorology. If possible, invite a meteorologist from the local television station or university to visit your classroom and describe the specifics of her or his job. What is most interesting about the position? What is most challenging? How would the individual advise young scientists who are interested in a career in meteorology?

Lightning

Stephen Kramer

Minneapolis, MN: Carolrhoda Books, 1992

Summary

This book is sure to amaze and inform. Using clear and precise text, the author provides young readers with an in-depth look at lightning and what scientists have discovered about this natural phenomenon. Students learn what lightning is, what happens during a lightning strike, how lightning is measured, how it is produced, different kinds of lightning, and basic safety tips. Filled with incredible photography by noted storm photographer Warren Faidley, this is one of the finest storm books available for any classroom or library.

Science Education Standards

The questions and activities in this section can be used to support teaching of the following content standards.

Science As Inquiry

> Abilities necessary to do scientific inquiry
> Understanding about scientific inquiry

Physical Science

> Light, heat, electricity, and magnetism
> Properties and changes of properties in matter
> Motions and forces
> Transfer of energy

Earth and Space Science

> Changes in Earth and sky

Science in Personal and Social Perspectives

> Personal health
> Natural hazards
> Risks and benefits

Critical Thinking Questions

1. What do you find most amazing about lightning?

2. After reading this book, what else would you like to know about lightning?

3.   Why must people be respectful of lightning?

4.   What are some good safety precautions to take during a thunderstorm?

5.   What scares you most about lightning?

Activities

1.   Near the end of the book, the author briefly explains an African legend about lightning. The legend involves a giant bird called Umpundulo. Share this brief description with students. Afterward, ask small groups to create their own original legend about lightning. What causes it, why is it so bright, why is it so brief, why is it so jagged? These are all questions that students can answer through legends of their own creation. Provide an opportunity for students to gather their legends together into a book or pamphlet for sharing with other classes.

2.   Invite students to log on to the following Web site: http://www.azstarnet.com/anubis/ zaphome.htm. This site has a great deal of information about lightning, including what it is and what makes it dangerous, as well as safety tips for home or school. Invite students to gather the necessary information and to create an informational brochure for students in a lower grade. What kind of information should they know? What would be the best way (without scaring them) to teach that information?

3.   An old saying is "lightning never strikes twice in the same spot." Invite students to contact several meteorologists or weather forecasters and ask them about the origin of that saying. What scientific evidence can they offer to disprove it? Be sure to provide sufficient opportunities for students to share their findings.

4.   After reading *Lightning,* students will know that the sudden movement of electrons causes this phenomenon from one place to another. This movement is so fast that the air around the electrons glows, illuminating a streak of lightning. The following activity will help students appreciate the interaction of negatively and positively charged electrons using another form of electricity—static.

   Sprinkle some pepper on top of a table. Ask one student to blow up a 9-inch balloon until it is the size of a child's head and then tie it off. Ask the student to rub the balloon on her or his head, a sweater or cotton shirt, or carpeting on the floor. Instruct the student to hold the balloon and slowly lower it over the sprinkled pepper. Students will note that as the balloon gets closer to the pepper, the grains of pepper will jump up to the surface of the balloon. This occurs because the surface of the balloon was given a negative charge when the student rubbed it. The pepper grains have a positive charge. Because opposites attract, the light grains of pepper "jump up" to the balloon when the distance between them is correct. Something similar happens in the generation of lightning.

5.   There are several safety rules people need to keep in mind during a lightning storm. These include:

   a.   Don't stand under a tree.

   b.   Move to low ground.

c. Don't swim, go boating, or participate in other water sports.

d. Don't use the telephone.

e. Don't touch the radio or telephone.

f. Don't use electrical appliances.

g. If caught outside, lie down.

Review these rules for students and invite several select groups to design and illustrate safety posters for display around the school.

6. Encourage students to log on to the following Web site: http://www.co.honolulu. hi.us/ocda/thunder.htm. They will learn much information about lightning, as well as safety rules that people should follow in the event of a lightning storm. Plan time to discuss this information with your students and ask them to share the data with their families.

7. If possible, obtain a copy of the National Geographic video *When Lightning Strikes* (catalog #FB52664; see Appendix C). Share this video with students and invite them to compare the information in the book with that in the video. Encourage them to create an oversized Venn diagram that displays important information from the book and significant data from the video. What similarities or difference do students note in these two productions?

8. Here's another activity that effectively demonstrates static electricity. Take a sheet of aluminum foil (approximately a 12-inch square). Fold it in half. Fold it in half two more times or until you have a strip of foil that is about 12 inches long and about $1\frac{1}{2}$ inches wide. Wrap the strip of aluminum foil around a bottle or other cylindrical object. Tape the ends together with a small piece of tape and slip the aluminum foil cylinder off the bottle. Place the cylinder so it's standing like a wheel on a smooth table. Fill a 9-inch balloon with air and tie it off. Rub the balloon in your hair, on a cotton shirt or sock, or on the carpeting. Move the balloon toward the aluminum foil cylinder, and it will begin to roll toward the balloon. (Note: Keep the balloon close to the cylinder, but don't allow it to touch. It is important that the aluminum foil cylinder is completely round. If it is slightly flat along one section, this activity will not work.) This activity works because the aluminum foil has a positive charge on its surface. When the balloon is rubbed or stroked, the electrons on its surface take on a negative charge. When the balloon is moved near the aluminum foil cylinder, the cylinder begins to roll toward the balloon because opposite charges attract. This is similar to the static electricity generated in lightning.

9. The author of *Lightning* is a classroom teacher in Vancouver, Washington. Your students may wish to learn about children's book authors and how they write their books. Invite students to log on to the Web site of the author of this resource book (who is also a teacher and has written several children's books) where they can learn about the process of writing: http://www.afredericks.com/author/index.html. If you or your students are interested in learning about children's authors who visit schools, you can log on to the following site for more information: http://www.snowcrest.net/kidpower/authors.html.

10. Invite students to create illustrations, diagrams, or mosaics of the different types of lightning: bead and rocket lightning, ribbon lightning, and ball lightning. To create a mosaic, instruct students to use various types of seeds, beans, split peas, rice, macaroni, and spices, which they can paint with watercolors. Have students hang their work throughout the room. They may also wish to create appropriate three-dimensional illustrations of the different types of thunderheads depicted in the book.

11. According to *Lightning,* the average lightning bolt is about 3 to 4 miles long and about 1 inch across. Ask students to measure the length of one roll of adding-machine tape (which is about 1 inch in width). Encourage them to calculate the number of rolls of adding machine tape that they would have to connect end to end to create a strip that was 3 to 4 miles long. Then, have students use a city map to calculate the distances between places in your town or community (e.g., the distance between the city park and a movie theater, the distance between the post office and the school). Encourage students to find two points in town that are between 3 and 4 miles apart and to plot them on the city map. Students may want to ride their bicycles (or have their parents drive them) between those two points to get a feel for the distance involved.

12. Students may be interested in seeing additional photographs and images of lightning. The following Web sites offer a variety of awe-inspiring images of lightning flashes:

    http://www.photolib.noaa.gov/lb_images/weather/lightning/light.htm

    http://www.photolib.noaa.gov/lb_images/nssl/lightn0.htm

13. Students also may be interested in viewing the following Web site, which was created by a young girl who was struck by lightning: http://www.azstarnet.com/anubis/zaphome.htm. After students have had an opportunity to view the site, take time to discuss the girl's experience and her suggestions for lightning safety.

Storm on the Desert

Carolyn Lesser

San Diego, CA: Harcourt Brace, 1997

Summary

Bright, lyrical text and soft illustrations make this a "must-have" book for any elementary classroom. Poetic language that sparkles with the intensity of the desert sun distinguishes this book as a perfect "read-aloud" addition to any study of storms. The author effectively captures the diversity of flora and fauna in the desert and then weaves those "life tales" into a story that grabs the imagination and captures the spirit of change that is part of the daily cycle of life in the Sonoran desert. Life before the storm, the rage of the storm itself, and the quiet that settles in the aftermath of the storm will mesmerize students time and time again. Ted Rand's evocative and rich watercolors highlight and complement this lyric poem to the majesty of the American Southwest.

Science Education Standards

The questions and activities in this section can be used to support teaching of the following content standards.

Science As Inquiry

Understanding about scientific inquiry

Life Science

Life cycles of organisms
Organisms and environments
Populations and ecosystems
Diversity and adaptations of organisms

Earth and Space Science

Changes in Earth and sky

Science in Personal and Social Perspectives

Changes in environment
Populations, resources, and environments

Critical Thinking Questions

1. How did this book change your mind about life in the desert?

2. Why is the storm such an important part of life in the desert?

3.   Which of the desert animals described in this book would you like to learn more about?

4.   How is the storm in this book similar to a storm that you have experienced?

5.   What did you enjoy most about the illustrations?

6.   What were some of the emotions you felt while reading (listening to) this book?

Activities

1.   Students may enjoy making their own rain. You will need a large glass jar, very hot tap water, 10 to 12 ice cubes, a foil pie pan, and a flashlight. Directions: Fill the jar halfway with very hot tap water. Fill the pie pan with ice cubes. Put it on top of the jar. Turn out the lights. Shine a flashlight into the jar. Invite students to note what happens inside the jar. After completing the experiment, students can record what happened and illustrate it step by step.

2.   Ask students to check an almanac for the yearly rainfall in your area. They can locate several cities in the United States and find the normal annual precipitation. Encourage students to compare the rainfall in several cities with that in your town or city, as well as that in selected towns in desert areas of the United States. They can plot this information on a large wall chart. Invite students to discuss the differences and similarities.

3.   Ask each student to imagine that she or he is a raindrop. Have them record their "life" as a raindrop from the moment they are created until they finally land on the Earth—in a puddle, on a plant or animal, or some other object. If you wish, ask students to imagine different types of adventures for their raindrops (e.g., blown about in a hurricane, landing on a dry dusty desert, freezing into a hailstone). Provide opportunities for students to share their stories in large group settings.

4.   Students may enjoy making their own homemade "rain sticks." Obtain several mailing tubes from the local post office or office supply store. Using a hammer and about 25 roofing nails, drive the nails through the tube at various angles and various locations up and down the tube (this part of the activity should only be done by an adult). Place a handful of dried beans inside a tube and replace the cap. Turn the tube upside down and the sound of the falling beans will sound like the patter of falling raindrops. Turn the tube over and over to repeat the process and the sounds.

5.   As an extension of Activity 4, invite students to create other homemade devices that simulate the sounds in a thunderstorm. For example, how could they create the sound of crackling lightning (a large tin sheet or saw bent back and forth) or the sound of thunder (a screwdriver with a fluted handle rolled back and forth over a wooden floor). You may wish to re-read the book aloud, inviting students to add the necessary sound effects.

6.   Have students maintain storm journals. As a storm begins to approach, ask them to record the events of that storm on an hourly basis. For example, what was the temperature, humidity, type of cloud cover, color of the sky, sounds, and so forth? They can record these observations in individual journals or in an oversized class journal for permanent display. When they have recorded several storms, invite students to discuss any similarities between selected storms.

7.   Invite students to write to one or more of the national parks listed below and request information about the flora and fauna that inhabit those special desert regions. When the brochures, flyers, leaflets, and descriptive information arrive invite students to assemble them into an attractive display in the classroom or a school display case.

> Death Valley National Park
> P.O. Box 579
> Death Valley, CA 92328
>
> Joshua Tree National Park
> 74485 National Park Drive
> Twentynine Palms, CA 92277
>
> Great Basin National Park
> Baker, NV 89311
>
> Big Bend National Park
> Big Bend, TX 79834

8.   Students may wish to visit a local gardening center or nursery. Invite them to purchase an inexpensive cactus plant. Invite them to carefully observe their cacti. What shape is it? Does the shape change as it grows? What do the needles look like? Students may wish to observe cactus features with a magnifying lens and record their observations in a desert journal.

9.   Students can keep up to date on the latest events, discoveries, and news about life in the deserts of the United States by accessing the Web site of *Desert USA Magazine* at http://www.desertusa.com. Here they can learn about the lives of the flora and fauna that inhabit U.S. deserts. They may wish to gather selected information, in the form of descriptive brochures or pamphlets, for the classroom library.

10.   Students may wish to take a virtual tour of a desert with the following Web site: org/MBGnet/sets/desert/index.htm. Here they will learn what a desert is like, what causes deserts, deserts of the world, desert plants and animals, and desert life at night. This wonderful site is full of incredible information.

11.   Divide the class into several groups and invite each one to plan a trip across the desert. Encourage each group to assemble a list of supplies and equipment they would need for their journey. What would be some essential items? What would they expect to see? Invite students to research the journeys of early pioneers who crossed the desert. Have students compare their information and post the lists on the bulletin board for whole-class discussions.

12.   Reading other books about the desert may interest your students. Following are several suggestions that your students will surely enjoy:

> Arnold, Caroline. (1990). *A Walk in the Desert.* Englewood Cliffs, NJ: Silver Press.
>
> Baker, Lucy. (1990). *Life in the Deserts.* New York: Franklin Watts.
>
> Hogan, Paula. (1991). *Expanding Deserts.* Milwaukee, WI: Gareth Stevens.

Siebert, Diane. (1988). *Mojave*. New York: HarperCollins.

Silver, Donald. (1995). *One Small Square: Cactus Desert*. New York: W. H. Freeman.

Twist, Clint. (1991). *Deserts*. New York: Dillon Press.

Wallace, Marianne. (1996). *America's Deserts*. Golden, CO: Fulcrum.

13.   The following Web site provides students with a description of the various types of clouds, characteristics of those clouds, and how rain forms: http://www.athena.ivy. nasa.gov/curric/weather/pricloud/index.html. After students have had an opportunity to view this site, encourage them to create an appropriate display (mural or poster) that illustrates cloud types.

Storms

Seymour Simon

New York: Mulberry Books, 1989

Summary

This wonderfully photographed book is filled with incredible information and facts about storms. Readers learn about how storms form, different types of storms around the world, and the effects storms have on various parts of the Earth. With intricate detail and his marvelous ability to capture the attention of any young scientist, Seymour Simon has crafted a book that will inform as well as delight. This is a book students will turn to again and again—not just for the amazing information, but also for the dynamic and awe-inspiring photography.

Science Education Standards

The questions and activities in this section can be used to support teaching of the following content standards.

Science As Inquiry

Abilities necessary to do scientific inquiry
Understanding about scientific inquiry

Physical Science

Transfer of energy

Earth and Space Science

Objects in the sky

Science in Personal and Social Perspectives

Changes in environments
Natural hazards
Risks and benefits

Critical Thinking Questions

1. Why should humans respect thunderstorms?

2. What have you learned about storms that you did not know before?

3. What is the most powerful thunderstorm you have experienced?

4. Why do so many thunderstorms occur around the world?

5. What are some safety precautions people should follow during a thunderstorm?

Activities

1. Ask students to gather newspaper and magazine articles about the weather or to bring in information from local broadcasts about violent storms in your area or from locations around the world. Students can file articles (and brief write-ups) in shoeboxes and share them in a "weather news" area. Encourage students to examine all the clippings and descriptions and compile a list comparing and contrasting the different storms around the country.

2. Many sayings and predictions about the weather have been handed down from one generation to the next. Following are two sayings or admonitions that have been passed down through the years:

   "Red sky at morning, sailor take warning. Red sky at night, sailors delight."

   "A January fog will freeze a hog."

   Invite students to look through other books and assemble a collection of weather sayings that have been handed down through the years. How accurate are those sayings? How do those sayings compare with actual meteorological events?

3. Because people did not always understand the weather, they have had many beliefs about the conditions or situations that cause weather patterns. Following are a few that people have had through the ages:

   Sea fog was once thought to be the breath of an underwater monster.

   In Germany, some people believed that a cat washed itself just before a shower of rain.

   The Aztecs believed that the Sun god could only be kept strong and bright through the use of human sacrifices.

   The Norse people thought that weather was created by the god Thor, who raced across the sky in a chariot pulled by two giant goats.

   Invite students to research other beliefs that people had about the weather. They may wish to collect their data from trade books, encyclopedias, or conversations with weather experts. Encourage them to put together a collection of these beliefs into a notebook or journal.

4. Many strange things have fallen from the sky as a result of unusual weather patterns. Students may want to research some of these unusual events and assemble them together into a notebook of "weird and wacky weather." Here are a few to get them started:

   On October 14, 1755, red snow fell on the Alps.

   In June 1940, a shower of silver coins fell on the town of Gorky, Russia.

   On June 16, 1939, it rained frogs at Trowbridge, England.

5. When severe weather is predicted for a specific area of the country (e.g., a hurricane along the Gulf Coast, a tornado in the plains states, severe thunderstorms in the Midwest) invite students to track the "history" of that storm. They may wish to consult the daily newspaper, a weekly newsmagazine, television or radio broadcasts, or firsthand accounts from meteorologists or weather forecasters. They can put together the "life story" of a storm in an album, including a variety of photos and news stories.

6. Write the names of various cities from around the United States on individual slips of paper. Place each piece of paper in an envelope. Ask each student to select a piece of paper randomly. Instruct students that they have now been designated the official rainfall recorder for that city. Using a variety of Web sites, newspaper accounts, or television news programs, invite each student to record the amount of rain that falls in that specific location over an extended period of time (one to three months). Afterward, encourage students to chart or graph their result to determine the cities that receive the most rainfall, the least rainfall, the most rainfall in 24 hours, or other predetermined categories. Plan time to discuss those charts.

7. Invite students to log on to the Web site http://www.nssl.noaa.gov/edu/ to learn about various types of storms. Encourage them to print and complete Billy and Maria's storm safety coloring book that is available from the Web site. When students finish, invite them to bind it into a book that they can keep for reference.

8. Divide students into groups and ask them to create a storm safety bulletin. Make use of literature and Web sites to get safety tips to use for the bulletin. Students should include precautions to take when preparing for a storm. Also, include tips for staying safe during a storm. Groups can distribute their bulletins to different classrooms in the school to use as a reference for storm safety.

9. Have students create a "question box" to be placed in the school lobby, where all students may leave questions they have about storms. Your students can answer these questions in writing and deliver them back to the students' classroom. From the questions received, students can compile a list of frequently asked questions and distribute them to the other classes in the school.

10. Provide students with copies of *USA Today* and ask them to cut out the weather maps on the back of the front section for a period of two weeks. Encourage students to examine the weather maps closely, noting the presence and movement of cold and warm fronts across the country. Invite students to list the kinds of weather changes the appearance of each front might bring and compare those with the actual weather conditions in succeeding days. Encourage students to compare weather found in various parts of the country.

11. Students may be interested in becoming "stormspotters." They can get up-to-the-minute information on the conditions and factors that contribute to storms through the following Web site: http://www.srh.noaa.gov/oun/skywarn/spotterguide.html. Here they will get information on various types of storms, a glossary of important terms, severe weather safety rules, and lots of photographs. After viewing this site, students may want to establish their own Stormspotter's Club. Members of the club can keep track of any severe weather pattern and make regular reports to the class or the entire school.

Thunder Cake

Patricia Pollaco

New York: Philomel Books, 1990

Summary

A loud clap of thunder booms and rattles the windows of the old farmhouse. Grandma proclaims "This is Thunder Cake baking weather." In short order, she and her granddaughter (who has always been afraid of thunderstorms and hides under the bed when they come) gather a variety of supplies and ingredients from around the farm. The storm gets closer and closer as the two whip up an ancestral recipe and get it into the oven before the storm arrives. Before long, they are enjoying a slice of cake and a cup of tea, even as the storm rages outside. This is a timeless tale of courage and understanding that will enhance and complement any study of storms. It's a book that will be read over and over again, by teachers and students alike!

Science Education Standards

The questions and activities in this section can be used to support teaching of the following content standards.

Science As Inquiry

Understanding about scientific inquiry

Physical Science

Light, heat, electricity, and magnetism
Transfer of energy

Earth and Space Science

Changes in Earth and sky

Science in Personal and Social Perspectives

Changes in environments
Natural hazards
Risks and benefits

History and Nature of Science

Nature of science

Critical Thinking Questions

1. Are you afraid of thunderstorms?

2.   Why are people afraid of thunderstorms?

3.   How did the grandmother know that Thunder Cake would help ease the granddaughter's fears?

4.   Which is scarier, thunder or lightning?

5.   What are some ways you handle your fears?

6.   Can you describe a recent thunderstorm that you remember?

Activities

1.   As a class, students may wish to create a weather dictionary containing all the weather words from *Thunder Cake.* They may wish to include a definition and illustration or find pictures in magazines or newspapers.

2.   Divide the class into groups. Invite each group to assemble a collection of amazing weather data or weather facts. For example:

> Lightning strikes the Earth as frequently as 100 times every second.
>
> In 1953, hailstones as big as golf balls fell in Alberta, Canada.
>
> In a blizzard, winds often reach speeds of 186 miles per hour.
>
> The wettest place in the world is a spot on the island of Kauai in the state of Hawaii. It rains more than 450 inches every year (that's more than 37 feet) on one mountaintop.
>
> The fastest tornado had a recorded speed of 280 miles per hour.

3.   Many local weather forecasters make visits to elementary classrooms as a regular part of their jobs. Contact your local TV station and inquire about scheduling a visit from the local weatherperson. Be sure students have an opportunity to generate some potential questions prior to the visit.

4.   Encourage students to create their own fables or folktales about specific weather patterns or events. They may wish to share these stories in a collection to be donated to the school library or to create a videotape that can be circulated to other classrooms in the school.

5.   In *Thunder Cake,* the grandmother teaches her granddaughter how to calculate the distance of a storm by counting the seconds from a strike of lightning to the sound of thunder (one second for each mile the storm is away). Amazingly, this rough calculation is remarkably accurate. Provide students with opportunities to engage in this calculation the next time a thunderstorm roars through your area. Depending on the time and location, you may be able to do this during school hours or encourage students to do the calculations at home (after school or on the weekend).

6.   In the back of the book is a recipe for "Thunder Cake." Work with your students in preparing this recipe. You may wish to duplicate the recipe and send it home with students so that they can share it with their families. Afterward, invite students to work with

their parents to find or create recipes for other natural disasters. For example, a family recipe for brownies (with small cracks in them) could be renamed "Earthquake Brownies"; a cookbook recipe for sugar cookies can be transformed into a recipe for "Tornado Snaps"; or a newspaper recipe for a mix of chocolate and vanilla pudding could be renamed "Hurricane Swirl." Invite students to gather several recipes together and develop them into a classroom cookbook to share with parents or other classes.

7. Have students imagine that they are going to describe a type of weather to someone who has never experienced it before, for example, a snowstorm to someone who lives near the equator. Encourage students to brainstorm a list of sentence starters such as:

> It looks like…
>
> It sounds like…
>
> It feels like…
>
> It makes you think of…

Then, invite students to "paint a picture" with words. How would they describe the event so that someone hearing it or reading it would know exactly what it was? Provide opportunities for students to post their descriptions on a section of the classroom bulletin board.

8. Encourage students to create an imaginary "thunderstorm emergency kit." Divide the class into several small groups and provide each group with a collection of old magazines. Invite each group to locate several different pictures, photos, or illustrations of items they would want to include in a kit. These could range from food items to emergency tools. After each group has selected a sampling of items, invite them to arrange the photos in a collage. Plan time for the groups to share their "kits" with each other.

9. Ask students to write letters to the young girl in the story. Encourage them to share hints that will help the girl be less fearful about thunderstorms. What ideas can they offer? Does it make any difference that they have never met the young girl? What ideas can they get from their parents or grandparents that they can share with the girl? Plan appropriate opportunities for students to share their letters.

10. Obtaining additional information about thunder and thunderstorms may interest your students. The following Web sites can provide them with a host of valuable data:

> http://members.home.net/jakasper/
>
> http://www.kings.k12.ca.us/central/cuesd.a/tq/weather/thunderlight.html

11. This simple activity will help students appreciate the creation of thunder. Blow up a lunch bag and tie the open end with a length of string. Place one hand on the top of the bag and the other on the bottom of the bag, then pop it. You have just created a miniature clap of thunder.

Sound is produced when something vibrates. When you popped the bag, it caused the air molecules to move quite rapidly. This sudden, rapid movement produces a sound. When a flash of lightning passes through the atmosphere, it heats the surrounding air, causing it to expand very quickly. It is this rapid movement that causes thunder. A short burst of lightning will often produce a short crash of thunder. Thunder rumbles or "rolls" when lightning covers a very large area or when obstructions, such as mountains or clouds, bounce the sounds around (causing echoes).

An Annotated Bibliography of Children's Literature

Note: All of the titles listed below were current and available at the time this book was written. Please check with your school or public library, local bookstore, wholesaler, or Internet bookseller (e.g., www.amazon.com or www.barnesandnoble.com) for availability and prices.

Volcanoes

Arnold, Eric. *Volcanoes! Mountains of Fire.* (New York: Random House, 1997).
    Young readers will learn how volcanoes "operate" and why they are some of nature's most amazing geological forces.

Clarke, Penny. *Volcanoes.* (New York: Franklin Watts, 1998).
    A brief but thorough over view of volcanoes around the world.

Farndon, John. *DK Pockets: Volcanoes.* (New York: DK Publishing, 1998).
    Small enough to carry in a pocket, this little treasure trove of information will satisfy any young volcanologist.

Griffey, Harriet. *Eyewitness Readers: Volcanoes and Other Natural Disasters.* (New York: DK Publishing, 2000).
    In the style that has made them famous, here is another delightful and engaging book from Eyewitness Readers—a great classroom resource.

Keane, Jo. *Volcanoes (Interfact).* (New York: World Book, 1998).
    Packed with facts and incredible information, this little book will delight and amaze any aspiring scientist.

Nelson, Sharlene. *Hawaii Volcanoes National Park.* (New York: Children's Press, 1998).
    Readers get an inside look at one of the most incredible national parks in the country, one established around an active volcano.

Nirgiotis, Nicholas. *Volcanoes: Mountains That Blow Their Tops.* (New York: Grosset & Dunlap, 1996).
    This is an easy-to-read introduction to seismic activity and volcanic power around the world.

Taylor, Barbara. *Mountains and Volcanoes.* (New York: Kingfisher, 1993).
A wonderfully illustrated text highlighted by informative details and stories about mountains and volcanoes

Vogt, Gregory. *Volcanoes.* (New York: Franklin Watts, 1993).
This is a perfect book for intermediate readers who are looking for a thorough and fact-filled exploration of volcanoes.

Walker, Sally. *Volcanoes: Earth's Inner Fire.* (Minneapolis, MN: Carolrhoda Books, 1994).
Impressive photographs and highly readable text distinguish this book as an essential part of any volcanic investigation.

Watt, Fiona. *Earthquakes and Volcanoes.* (Tulsa, OK: EDC Publishing, 1993).
Colorful and descriptive illustrations and loads of amazing facts make this book a perfect compliment to any volcano study.

Zoehfeld, Kathleen. *How Mountains Are Made.* (New York: HarperCollins, 1995).
Mountain formation is described through the eyes of four children.

Earthquakes

Bain, Iain. *Mountains and Earth Movements.* (New York: Franklin Watts, 1984).
What are the effects of erosion, weathering, faulting, folding, and continental drift on the creation of mountains? This book describes all of them in detail.

Farndon, John. *How the Earth Works: 100 Ways Parents and Kids Can Share the Secrets of the Earth.* (New York: Readers Digest, 1992).
This text includes experiments and projects designed to help kids learn about the Earth.

Green, Jen. *Read About Earthquakes.* (Brookfield, CT: Millbrook Press, 2000).
This book offers younger readers basic, clear information about the nature and power of earthquakes.

Levy, Matthys. *Earthquake Games: Earthquake and Volcanoes Explained by Games and Experiments.* (New York: McElderry Books, 1997).
This fabulous books takes a game-like approach to earthquakes and volcanoes. Great illustrations and lots of fun highlight this valuable resource.

Loeschnig, Louis. *Simple Earth Science Experiments with Everyday Materials.* (New York: Sterling, 1996).
Dozens of explorations, discoveries, and experiments designed to help youngsters learn more about their planet.

Morris, Neil. *Earthquakes.* (Hauppage, NY: Barron's, 1999).
This book effectively blends simplicity with entertainment to offer young readers a real appreciation for geological forces.

Pope, Joyce. *Earthquakes.* (Brookfield, CT: Copper Beech, 1998).
Colorful illustrations and lots of factual information make this book a worthwhile addition to the natural disasters library.

Sattler, Helen. *Our Patchwork Planet.* (New York: Lothrop, Lee & Shepard, 1995).
This book provides the reader with an interesting excursion through present-day tectonic theory.

Silverstein, Alvin, and Virginia Silverstein. *Plate Tectonics.* (New York: Twenty-First Century Books, 1998).
This book provides a brief overview of plate tectonics and how that theory has contributed to our understanding of earthquakes.

Sipiera, Paul. *Earthquakes.* (New York: Children's Press, 1998).
Basic information and descriptive photographs are hallmarks of this book, which is part of a series.

Spies, Karen. *Earthquakes (When Disaster Strikes).* (New York: Twenty-First Century Books, 1995).
The information here is well-presented, accurate, and informative for intermediate-level students.

Stidworthy, John. *Earthquakes and Volcanoes.* (New York: Silver Dolphin, 1996).
This book describes how natural forces can raise mountains, build islands, and change the weather. A good overview of natural phenomena.

Sutherland, Lin. *Earthquakes and Volcanoes.* (Pleasantville, NY: Readers Digest, 2000).
Complete information and descriptive photographs provide readers with background data on earthquakes and volcanoes.

Walker, Sally. *Earthquakes.* (Minneapolis, MN: Carolrhoda Books, 1996).
Full of information and mesmerizing photographs, this book admirably explains complex geological forces without oversimplification.

Floods and Tsunamis

Allaby, Michael. *Floods (Dangerous Weather Series).* (New York: Facts on File, 1997).
Clean, clear information on the power and destructiveness of floods highlight this book.

Armbruster, Ann. *Floods.* (New York: Franklin Watts, 1996).
This text is a thorough introduction to one of nature's most devastating powers and is filled with important information.

Badt, Karin. *The Mississippi Flood of 1993.* (New York: Children's Press, 1997).
Readers get an opportunity to look at the "birth" of a flood and the havoc its causes during one summer in the Midwest.

Buck, Pearl. *The Big Wave.* (New York: Harper & Row, 1986).
 This is a classic tale of two boys in Japan and how they deal with the power and sorrow of a tsunami. A magnificent read-aloud book!

Flaherty, Michael. *Tidal Waves and Flooding.* (Brookfield, CT: Copper Beech Books, 1998).
 This book (with its incorrect title) provides brief explanations on the destructiveness of floods, tsunamis, and hurricanes.

Hiscock, Bruce. *The Big Rivers: The Missouri, the Mississippi, and the Ohio.* (New York: Atheneum, 1997).
 This book focuses on the world's third largest tidal basin and how these three rivers influence the lives of the people who live near them.

Rozens, Alexander. *Floods (When Disaster Strikes).* (New York: Twenty-First Century Books, 1995).
 Compelling text and an abundance of photos make this book a good introduction to the incredible power of flooding.

Sipiera, Paul, and Diane Sipiera. *Floods.* (New York: Children's Press, 1998).
 A good resource for intermediate-level readers. The authors provide young scientists with the basics about, and destructiveness of, floods.

Hurricanes

Green, Jen. *Hurricanes and Typhoons (Closer Look At).* (Brookfield, CT: Copper Beech Books, 1998).
 The author provides readers with inside information on hurricanes, typhoons, cyclones, tornadoes, and twisters along with basic safety information.

Greenberg, Keith. *Hurricanes and Tornadoes (When Disaster Strikes).* (New York: Twenty-First Century Books, 1995).
 Fascinating information and intriguing data permeate this addition to a study of natural disasters.

Hood, Susan. *Hurricanes (The Weather Channel).* (New York: Simon Spotlight, 1998).
 How do hurricanes get their name? Where do they form? Which was the worst in history? The author answers these questions (and more) in this book.

Llewellyn, Claire. *Wild, Wet and Windy.* (Cambridge, MA: Candlewick Press, 1997).
 This book is a colorful and fact-filled book all about hurricanes, tornadoes, monsoons, lightning, and avalanches. A great introduction to natural disasters.

Morgan, Sally. *Read About Hurricanes.* (Brookfield, CT: Millbrook Press, 2000).
 Short, pithy text and informative details highlight this brief overview of nature's destructive powers.

Tornadoes

Claybourne, Anna. *Read About Tornadoes*. (Brookfield, CT: Millbrook Press, 2000).
> A brief overview of tornadoes accompanied by interesting photography makes this a good introduction to tornadoes.

Herman, Gail. *Storm Chasers: Tracking Twisters*. (New York: Grosset & Dunlap, 1997).
> This is a fictionalized story about two storm chasers and how they study and research tornadoes out in the field.

Kahl, Jonathan. *Storm Warning: Tornadoes and Hurricanes*. (Minneapolis, MN: Lerner Publications, 1993).
> An authoritative text filled with dynamic photography, this book is perfect for intermediate readers who are looking for precise information.

Lampton, Christopher. *Tornado (A Disaster Book)*. (Brookfield, CT: Millbrook Press, 1994).
> A thorough and compelling text takes older readers inside the fury and power of tornadoes. This book also includes safety measures.

Murray, Peter. *Tornadoes*. (Chanhassen, MN: The Child's World, 1999).
> Short paragraphs answer student's basic questions about tornadoes—where they happen, how they form, and the damage they cause.

Penner, Lucille. *Twisters*. (New York: Random House, 1996).
> A good introduction to tornadoes for readers in the second or third grade, this book is filled with amazing facts and heart-stopping terrors.

Avalanches and Landslides

Merrick, Patrick. *Avalanches (Forces of Nature Series)*. (Chanhassen, MN: The Child's World, 1998).
> A thorough and complete overview of the horror and immense power of avalanches. The text also provides safety rules.

Storms

DeWitt, Linda. *What Will the Weather Be?* (New York: HarperCollins, 1991).
> This brief book is a wonderful introduction to meteorologists, the instruments they use and what they measure, and weather patterns and changes.

Erlbach, Arlene. *Blizzards*. (New York: Children's Press, 1997).
> One of the few children's books to deal with this topic, the author convincingly offers readers basic information on the dangers of these storms.

Gibbons, Gail. *Weather Words and What They Mean*. (New York: Holiday House, 1990).
> A terrific book that introduces young readers to common meteorologic terms and their definitions.

Markle, Sandra. *A Rainy Day.* (New York: Orchard Books, 1993).
> An illustrated explanation of why it rains, what happens when it does, and where the rain goes.

McMillan, Bruce. *The Weather Sky.* (New York: Farrar, Straus, and Giroux, 1991).
> This book presents a year's worth of sky changes, along with color photographs and descriptive illustrations.

McVey, Vicki. *The Sierra Club Book of Weatherwisdom.* (San Francisco: Sierra Club, 1991).
> Basic weather principles and experiments in tandem with weather customs and traditions highlight this book.

Rosado, Maria. *Blizzards and Ice Storms.* (New York: Simon & Schuster, 1999).
> This is a rich and thoroughly researched book filled with facts, experiments, survival tips, and many photos.

Simon, Seymour. *Lightning.* (New York: William Morrow, 1997).
> With his usual clear and concise text accompanied by dynamic and exciting photos, Simon shares the mysteries of lightning with young readers.

Steele, Philip. *Rain: Causes and Effects.* (New York: Franklin Watts, 1991).
> An excellent introduction to rain and its effects on humans. Includes several simple experiments.

Wyatt, Valerie. *Weatherwatch.* (Reading, MA: Addison-Wesley, 1990).
> A book packed with weather lore, weather facts, weather data, and loads of experiments.

Web Sites

The following Web sites can provide you with valuable background information, a wealth of science resources, scores of up-to-date lesson plans, and numerous tools for expanding any unit or lesson on natural disasters. They can become important adjuncts to any literature-based science curriculum and can be used by teachers and students alike. Use them to keep your lessons and units fresh and up-to-date.

Note: These Web sites were current and accurate at the time of publication. Please be aware that some may change, others may be eliminated, and new ones will be added to the various search engines that you use at home or at school.

General

http://www.nsta.org

This is the home page for the National Science Teachers Association (NSTA), the professional organization for all teachers of science.

http://www.afredericks.com

This Web site is designed to provide busy classroom teachers with the best resources in elementary science. It has many exciting ideas.

http://lcweb.loc.gov/coll/print/guide/

The Library of Congress has thousands of images that are available for downloading. A keyword search index helps in locating images appropriate to any area of the science curriculum.

http://www.si.edu

The Smithsonian Institution is a repository of thousands and thousands of resources for any and all elements of elementary science.

http://www.askanexpert.com/askanexpert/

This site will provide you and your students with opportunities to ask questions of specific experts in various areas.

http://server2.greatlakes.k12.mi.us/

This site provides an incredible collection of teacher resources available for downloading. Included are lesson plans, computer software, HyperCard files, news resources, thematic units, guest speakers, field trips, and student-created material resources.

http://www.teachers.net/lessons/

Take a lesson, leave a lesson at the Teachers Net Lesson Exchange. The lessons cover all subjects and grade levels, and the site includes links to the teachers who posted the lessons.

http://www.pacificnet.net/~mandel/

A wonderful place to share ideas, concerns, and questions with educators from around the world. The material is updated weekly, and you'll be able to obtain lesson plans in every curricular area. Also included are teaching tips for both new and experienced teachers.

http://www.enc.org

This is the Eisenhower National Clearinghouse for Math and Science Education and includes detailed descriptions of curriculum materials, articles from professional journals on science teaching, and favorite Internet sites for teachers. This is a super site!

Children's Literature Sites

http://www.acs.ucalgary.ca/~dkbrown

This is the ultimate compendium of literature resources. It includes book awards, authors on the Web, book reviews, recommended books, book discussion groups, children's literature organizations, best sellers, and scores of teaching ideas.

http://www.carolhurst.com/

This site has a wonderful collection of reviews of great books for kids, ideas of ways to use them in the classroom, and collections of books and activities about particular subjects, curricular areas, themes, and professional topics.

http://www.scils.rutgers.edu/special/kay/childlit.html

At this site, you'll find resources and valuable information on how to effectively use children's literature in the classroom. The focus is on multiple genres and various methods for promoting good books to all ages and all abilities.

http://www.users.interport.net/~fairrosa/

Here are articles, reviews, lists, links, authors, discussions, and monthly updates about the best in children's literature and how to share it with kids. This is a great site for the always-busy classroom teacher.

http://www.ipl.org

This is the Internet Public Library, an overwhelming assembly of collections and resources of a large public library. The site covers just about every topic in children's literature with an incredible array of resources.

http://www.ccn.cs.dal.ca/~aa331/childlit.html#review

This site is dedicated to reviewing Web resources related to children's literature and youth services. The resources are aimed toward school librarians, children's writers, illustrators, book reviewers, storytellers, parents, and teachers.

http://i-site.on.ca/booknook.html
This site is a repository of book reviews for kids written by other kids. The reviews are categorized by grade level: K–3, 4–6, 7–9, and 10–12. It's a great way to find out what's popular among young readers.

http://www.armory.com/~web/notes.html
This site provides reviews of children's literature written by teachers and others who love kid's books. It's an electronic journal of book reviews concentrating on how well books are written and how well they entertain.

Natural Disaster Sites

http://ltpwww.gsfc.nasa.gov/ndrd/disaster/links/Type/
WOW—what a Web site! If you only have time to look at one site, make it this one. It has links to most of the other major Web sites on disasters around the world. This is a great starting place for teachers and students.

http://www.ngdc.noaa.gov/seg/fliers/se-0801.shtml#tsuslides
This site is a catalog of slides available from National Oceanic and Atmospheric Administration featuring various natural disasters including earthquakes, hurricanes, tsunamis, and volcanoes. A super resource!

http://www.yahooligans.com/content/ka/almanac/disaster/index.html
At this site students can learn about a wide variety of natural disasters from around the world and throughout history.

http://www.ngdc.noaa.gov/cgi-bin/seg/m2h?seg/haz_volume3.men
On this site, students will be able to view photographs of damage caused by several different types of natural disasters.

http://library.thinkquest.org/J003007/Disasters2/menu/menu1.htm
Here, students will learn about volcanoes, tsunamis, hurricanes, and earthquakes in Hawaii.

http://www.discovery.com/news/earthalert/earthalert.html
Students can get daily updates on natural disasters around the world on this site. It is a great addition to any natural disaster unit.

http://disasterium.com
This site provides students with a day-by-day listing of natural disasters around the world. Another fantastic complement to a natural disaster unit.

http://www.germantown.k12.il.us/html/title.html
This site has a variety of facts, pictures, and links about natural disasters. Different types of geological and meteorological disasters are profiled.

http://library.thinkquest.org/J001382F/main.htm
This is one of my all-time favorite sites. It includes an enormous amount of information on volcanoes, earthquakes, and tornadoes. Be sure to turn up the volume for some great sounds!

Science Lesson Plans

http://www.digicity.com/lesson/l_socstd.html
>If you're looking for more than 2,600 lesson plans in a variety of subject areas and across the grades, this is your site.

http://www.col-ed.org/cur/#sst1
>A magnificent array of various lesson plans from the Columbia Education Center (Portland, Oregon) is available at this site.

http://www.lessonplanspage.com/indexmain.htm
>This site has more than 900 free lesson plans in a wide variety of subjects and areas.

http://www.col-ed.org/cur/science.html
>Teachers from around the country created these lesson plans for use in their own classrooms. The site includes many science lessons.

http://www.csun.edu/~vceed009/lesson.html
>This site includes a compendium of lesson plans sites from an incredible variety of sources. Outstanding!

http://www.teachersfirst.com/lesn-sci.htm
>If you're looking for content-rich lesson plans, experiments, projects, and activities from a host of sources, this is your site.

http://www.techplus.com/scipage/lessons.htm
>Science lesson plans from across the country are included on this site.

Virtual Field Trips

http://dreamscape.com/frankvad/museums.html
>Take your students on more than 300 virtual tours of selected museums, exhibits, and points of special interest around the world.

http://www.field-guides.com
>You and your students can take a variety of field trips around the country with this site.

http://homeschoolfaq.com/online_field_trips.htm
>There are an abundance of places to visit on this all-inclusive site. This is a great resource for homework and out-of-class assignments.

http://www.uen.org/utahlink/tours/
>Your class can visit educational locations, create and edit your own field trips, and get links to other virtual field trips on the Web.

Video Resources

It is hoped that few students in your classroom will be witness to or involved in a natural disaster. Nonetheless, they can view the force, intensity, and destructive powers of these natural phenomena through a variety of classroom and instructional videos. Videos offer your students eyewitness, firsthand accounts of recent and historical natural disasters. Students will be able to observe a natural disaster in all its intensity and gain a newfound appreciation for these incredible occurrences.

The following list includes a selection of videos to use in conjunction with a natural disaster lesson or unit. It is wise to view videos before showing them to students, which will provide you with the necessary background to respond to questions and to direct classroom discussions.

All of the videos listed below were current and available at the time of the writing of this book. Those preceded by (A) are available through Amazon.com (http://www.amazon.com), those preceded by (NG) are available through the National Geographic Society (http:// www. nationalgeographic.com), and those preceded by (D) are available through the Discovery Channel (http://www.discovery.com). You may also be able to rent or purchase these videos (as well as any new releases) at your local video store.

Volcanoes

(A) *America's Most Deadly Volcanoes* (ASIN: B00000643L)
(A) *Extreme Disasters: Real Volcanoes* (ASIN: 1575234149)
(A) *Eyewitness: Volcano* (ASIN: 6304165323)
(NG) *In the Shadow of Vesuvius* (#51353C)
(A) *Inside Hawaiian Volcanoes* (ASIN: 63033579469)
(D) *Raging Planet: Volcano* (#123612)
(A) *The Story of America's Great Volcanoes* (ASIN: 1568553986)
(NG) *Volcano* (#51411C)
(A) *Volcanoes* (ASIN: 6302617650)
(A) *Volcanoes of the Deep* (ASIN: 630537337X)
(A) *World's Most Dangerous Volcanoes* (ASIN: B00000644G)

Earthquakes

(A) *Earthquake: Death & Destruction* (ASIN: 6304816979)
(D) *Great Quakes* (#738534)
(A) *Great San Francisco Earthquake* (ASIN: 6302431913)
(NG) *Natural Disasters* (#FB50594)
(NG) *Nature's Fury* (#51993C)

(NG) *Our Dynamic Earth* (#FB51162)
(A) *San Francisco—Earthquake!* (ASIN: 6301562305)
(NG) *When the Earth Quakes* (#FB52542)

Floods and Tsunamis

(NG) *Can't Drown This Town* (#FB58013)
(A) *Floods* (ASIN: 6305641161)
(NG) *Killer Wave: Power of the Tsunami* (#51904C)
(A) *Nature's Fury: Flood* (ASIN: 6304946430)
(A) *Nova—Flood* (ASIN: 6304096755)
(D) *Raging Planet: Fire and Flood* (#720128)
(D) *Raging Planet: Tidal Wave* (#113167)

Hurricanes

(NG) *After the Hurricane* (#FB58012)
(NG) *Cyclone* (#50901C)
(A) *Deadly Hurricanes* (ASIN: 6304575084)
(A) *Hurricanes—Deadly Wind* (ASIN: B000006QZF)
(A) *Nova—Hurricane* (ASIN: 6304462921)
(D) *Raging Planet: Hurricane* (#113159)

Tornadoes

(A) *The Chasers of Tornado Alley* (ASIN: 0965074501)
(A) *Nova—Tornado* (ASIN: 6304463235)
(A) *Secrets of the Unknown—Tornadoes* (ASIN: 630207763X)
(A) *Tornado Chasers* (ASIN: 6303584225)
(A) *Tornadoes! THE ENTITY* (ASIN: 0928519015)

Avalanches and Landslides

(A) *Avalanche* (ASIN: B0000036J8)
(NG) *Avalanche: The White Death* (#70040C)
(A) *Avalanche—White Walls of Dust* (ASIN: B000006QZG)
(D) *Landslide: Gravity Kills* (#164178)
(D) *Raging Planet: Avalanche* (#113126)
(NG) *Thunder on the Mountain: Landslides and Avalanches* (#70034C)

Storms

(A) *Chasing Killer Storms* (ASIN: B00000I1M9)
(D) *Raging Planet: Blizzard* (#123638)
(D) *Raging Planet: Lightning* (#113134)
(NG) *Storm of the Century* (#70015C)
(NG) *Where Storms Begin* (#FB528130
(NG) *When Lightning Strikes* (#FB52664)

Other Natural Occurrences

If there is one constant in the world it is that the Earth is dynamic—always in a state of change, always in a state of transition. The world we live in is never static, but rather evolves or is changed in a wide variety of ways.

Throughout the world, there are natural occurrences that happen all the time. Many of these are taken for granted; others are somewhat unpredictable or random. A natural occurrence may be as silent and unseen as a drought that slowly takes over a portion of the world affecting millions of lives for several years. Or it may be as sudden as a brief summer hailstorm. Whatever the event or circumstances, we know that these occurrences are a natural part of our world.

When a natural occurrence results in death, destruction, or damage (widespread or local), then it turns into a natural disaster. A lightning strike in a remote wooded area of Colorado may result in a brief fire that quickly burns itself out. Or, it may result in a forest fire of enormous proportions that spreads over thousands of acres of forestland or populated areas in a dozen states. The first event is a natural occurrence, the second a natural disaster.

As evidenced by the literature and activities throughout this book, natural disasters effect human life in myriad ways. Widespread carnage or physical devastation is usually the result of a natural disaster (although not always). Large geographical areas may be effected, and the landscape may be altered temporarily or permanently.

This appendix lists several natural occurrences that your students may wish to investigate as part of an extended unit or series of lessons on natural disasters. You are encouraged to share these events with your class and invite them to conduct their own independent research on the scientific facts behind these events, as well as places around the world where these occurrences take place.

Forest Fires

Forest fires are a natural part of the landscape. They are a way the forest renews, regenerates and replenishes itself. Many organisms are dependent on fires in order to survive. Several species of plants cannot germinate without a forest fire.

However, forest fires are also destructive. They sweep across the landscape with no regard for life or property and can destroy entire neighborhoods in a matter of minutes. Humans who have encroached on the natural environment often suffer the consequences of a devastating and often natural forest fire.

Literature

Frasier, Mary Ann. *Forest Fire!* (Mahweh, NJ: Troll, 1999).
>   A delightfully illustrated book that describes the healthy role of forest fires in all ecosystems.

Lauber, Patricia. *Summer of Fire: Yellowstone 1988.* (New York: Orchard, 1991).
>   This fascinating book is filled with photographs of Yellowstone Park before, during, and after the devastating fires of 1988. The emphasis in this book is on fire as a renewing process.

Patent, Dorothy Hinshaw. *Fire: Friend or Foe?* (New York: Clarion, 1998).
>   This is a terrific book that describes and explains forest fires and their importance in the balance of nature.

Pringle, Laurence. *Fire in the Forest.* (New York: Atheneum, 1995).
>   This will enlighten readers and provide them with valuable information about this very natural phenomenon.

Web Sites

http://www.germantown.k12.il.us/html/wildfires.html
>   A great site created by seventh-grade students in Illinois. A lot of information and several interesting photos highlight this site about wildfires.

http://www.sover.net/~kenandeb/fire/hotshot.html
>   A "Hot Shot Photo Journal" follows a U.S. Forest Service Hotshot Crew as they fight forest fires in America's wilderness.

http://www.smokeybear.com/
>   The "Smokey Bear" site provides information on how people can help prevent forest fires.

Blizzards

A blizzard is actually a snowstorm but on a much grander scale. By definition, a blizzard is a combination of falling or blowing snow propelled by sustained winds of at least 35 miles per hour for at least three hours and which limits visibility to ¼ mile or less. The temperature is typically below 32 degrees.

Some of the world's worst blizzards occur in Antarctica. Here, strong winds can blow snow with such ferocity and power that visibility is reduced to near zero and survival is measured in minutes, not hours.

Literature

Erlbach, Arlene. *Blizzards.* (New York: Children's Press, 1997).
>   A simple, yet thorough, explanation of blizzards highlights this informative and engaging book.

Hopping, Lorraine. *Wild Weather: Blizzards*. (New York: Cartwheel, 1999).
> This book describes several memorable blizzards as well as the weather conditions that create them.

Murphy, Jim. *Blizzard*. (New York: Scholastic, 2000).
> This book is a thorough and complete introduction to blizzards and their effects on humans.

Rosado, Maria. *Blizzards and Ice Storms*. (New York: Simon & Schuster, 1999).
> In this brief but engaging book, students learn what makes a blizzard blow, how ice storms form, and when the worst snowstorms in U.S. history occurred. A lot of fun facts and photographs.

Web Sites

http://www.germantown.k12.il.us/html/blizzard1.html
> Lots of information about blizzards can be found on this site created by students. A wind chill chart provides useful data for those living in colder regions of the country.

http://www.yahooligans.com/content/ka/almanac/disaster/dis00004.html
> This is a brief site that provides students with basic information about blizzards and hailstorms. Some of the most memorable ones throughout history are also listed on this site.

http://weathereye.kgan.com/expert/blizzard/WinterSafe.html
> This informative site provides students (and their parents) with valuable information on how to stay safe during the winter months.

http://www.srh.noaa.goc/oun/severewx/safety.html
> This site has valuable information on how to be safe and protect yourself during severe weather such as a blizzard.

Hailstorms

A hailstorm can cause enormous damage. Hailstones (actually small chunks of ice) can beat down plants, kill small animals, and severely injure humans. Property damage can be quite extensive during a hailstorm.

Hailstones form when water droplets in the atmosphere surround tiny particles of dust or ice. These droplets freeze to the particles and are tossed around inside thunderclouds. As they are tossed around, they grow larger and larger as more water freezes to them. When these frozen droplets get too large, they fall to the ground as hailstones.

Literature

Branley, Franklyn. *Rain and Hail*. (New York: HarperCollins, 1983).
> A simple explanation of the water cycle including clouds, rain, and hail is the emphasis in this easy-to-read book.

Web Sites

http://www.srh.noaa.gov/oun/skywarn/spotterguide.html
> This site provides a wealth of information about how to spot various types of severe storms.

http://www.photolib.noaa.gov/
> The NOAA Photo Library has loads of photographs of the effects of severe weather in different regions of the country. This is a perfect site for downloading photos for school reports.

Drought

Basically a drought is a severe lack of water in a particular area. Scientifically, there are three different types of droughts. One is when there is a lack of rainfall over a long period of time. This type of drought occurs in areas that receive a predictable amount of rain each year (as opposed to a desert). The second type of drought occurs in areas that have critically low levels of groundwater and reduced water flow in rivers and streams. The third type of drought is known as an agricultural drought and is typically associated with extended periods of extreme heat. This results in less water available for crops.

The worst drought in U.S. history occurred between 1931 and 1938. Spreading over the Great Plains states it created a condition now known as the Dust Bowl. Thousands of farmers lost their crops and thousands more moved from this area to other parts of the country.

Africa has been visited by droughts more frequently than any other continent.

Web Sites

http://users.netlink.com.au/~jhallett/drought.htm
> At this site students will obtain a very brief explanation of droughts and some of the most significant ones to effect the world during the twentieth century.

http://www.germantown.k12.il.us/html/droughts1.html
> This is a great site created by a group of seventh-grade students. A lot of information about droughts around the world can be found on this engaging site.

http://www.discovery.com/area/history/dustbowl/dustbowl1.2.html
> This site (created by the Discovery Channel) provides students with some interesting insight into the Dust Bowl conditions of the 1930s.

http://www.yahooligans.com/content/ka/almanac/disaster/dis00005.html
> This site provides brief definitions of droughts and famines. Also included are some of the most devastating droughts and famines from throughout history.

Global Warming

Over the course of the last two decades, the Earth has gotten warmer. Many scientists say that this is the result of the Greenhouse Effect. This is a natural occurrence in which the Earth's atmosphere allows light from the sun to pass through and heat the Earth's surface. Gases, such as carbon dioxide, absorb the returning heat and also warm the surface. Without this effect, life on the Earth would cease to exist.

However, humans have created conditions that are leading to an overall increase in world-wide temperatures. This is due primarily to the release of increased levels of carbon dioxide into the atmosphere. This is the result of air pollution, deforestation, farming methods, and the burning of fossil fuels such as coal, gas, and oil. Industry and automobiles are the chief producers of elevated levels of carbon dioxide. With more carbon dioxide in the atmosphere, the Earth becomes warmer and warmer.

Literature

Edmonds, Alex. *The Greenhouse Effect*. (Brookfield, CT: Copper Beech, 1997).
> This book provides readers with important information about greenhouse gasses, weather, and global warming. It's filled with loads of illustrations, charts, graphs, and pictures.

Hawkes, Nigel. *Climate Crisis*. (Brookfield, CT: Millbrook, 2000).
> This book is a thorough and engaging look at global warming with a focus on its causes as well as its prevention.

Johnson, Rebecca. *Greenhouse Effect*. (Minneapolis, MN: Lerner, 1991).
> Readers will learn about the causes of global warming as well as its effects on geography and the environment. The explanations are detailed and clear.

Web Sites

http://www.epa.gov/globalwarming/index.html
> This is an extensive site that provides students with a complete and thorough introduction to global warming. There's a lot to learn here!

http://ksd.marin.k12.ca.us/KMS/oldprojects/Warming/gw_kauf.html
> At this site students can learn about global warming and the Greenhouse Effect from middle school students.

http://www.enviroweb.org/edf/
> Here, students can learn all about global warming and how it can be stopped.

http://www.edf.org/pubs/Brochures/GlobalWarming/
> Created by the American Museum of Natural History, this site offers students loads of information about global warming and the Greenhouse Effect.

http://www.pbs.org/wgbh/warming/
> Created by PBS, "What's Up with the Weather" is an all-inclusive and rich site that has lots of great information for every student (and their parents).

Appendix E

Teacher Resources
by Anthony D. Fredericks

Note: All of the following books are available from Teacher Ideas Press (P.O. Box 6633, Englewood, CO 80155; 1-800-237-6124; http://www.lu.com/tip).

Frantic Frogs and Other Frankly Fractured Folktales for Readers Theatre [ISBN: 1-56308-174-1]. (123 pages; $19.50)

Have you heard "Don't Kiss Sleeping Beauty, She's Got Really Bad Breath" or "The Brussels Sprouts Man (The Gingerbread Man's Unbelievably Strange Cousin)"? This resource (grades 4–8) offers 30 reproducible satirical scripts for rip-roaring dramatics. Side-splitting send-ups and wacky folktales are guaranteed to bring snickers, chuckles, and belly laughs into the classroom.

The Integrated Curriculum: Books for Reluctant Readers, Grades 2–5 (2d Edition) [ISBN: 0-87287-994-1]. (220 pages; $22.50)

This book presents guidelines for motivating students and using literature with reluctant readers. It contains more than 40 book units on titles carefully selected to motivate the most reluctant readers, such as *The Three Bears*, *The Salamander Room*, and *Sky Tree*. Each unit includes a summary, discussion questions that foster critical thinking, and cross-curricular extensions.

Involving Parents Through Children's Literature: P–K [ISBN: 1-56308-022-2]. (86 pages; $15.00)

Involving Parents Through Children's Literature: Grades 1–2 [ISBN: 1-56308-012-5]. (95 pages; $14.50)

Involving Parents Through Children's Literature: Grades 3–4 [ISBN: 1-56308-013-3]. (96 pages; Out of Print)

Involving Parents Through Children's Literature: Grades 5–6 [ISBN: 1-56308-014-1]. (107 pages; Out of Print)

This series of four books stimulates parent participation in the learning process. Reproducible activity sheets based on quality children's books are designed in a convenient format so children can take them home. Each sheet includes a book summary, discussion questions, and engaging activities for adults and children that stimulate comprehension and promote reading enjoyment.

The Librarian's Complete Guide to Involving Parents Through Children's Literature: Grades K-6 [ISBN: 1-56308-538-0]. (137 pages; $24.50)

Activities for 101 children's books are presented in a reproducible format, so librarians can distribute them to students to take home and share with parents. Each sheet includes a book summary, discussion questions, and a list of learning activities for parents to do with their children. These projects build strong bonds of communication between parents and children.

More Social Studies Through Children's Literature: An Integrated Approach [ISBN: 1-56308-761-8]. (225 pages; $27.50)

Energize your social studies curriculum with dynamic, "hands-on, minds-on" projects based on such great children's books as *Amazing Grace*, *Fly Away Home*, and *Lon Po Po*. This book offers hundreds of activities designed to stimulate and engage students in positive learning and help teachers implement national (and many state) standards. Each of the 33 units has book summaries, social studies topic areas, critical thinking questions, and dozens of easy-to-do activities for every grade level. This book is a perfect complement to the earlier *Social Studies Through Children's Literature: An Integrated Approach*, and it effectively builds upon the success of that volume.

Readers Theatre for American History [ISBN: 1-56308-860-6]. (ca. 234 pages; $30.00).

This book offers a participatory approach to American history. The 25 scripts stimulate students to become active participants in several historical events. Students will work alongside Father Junipero Serra at Mission San Juan Capistrano; they'll stand alongside Thomas Jefferson as he drafts the Declaration of Independence; they'll travel with a Midwestern family as they trek across the Oregon Trail; and they'll travel with Neal Armstrong in his history-making trip to the Moon. In short, students will get a "you are there" perspective of the unfolding of critical milestones and memorable circumstances that have shaped the American experience.

Science Adventures with Children's Literature: A Thematic Approach [ISBN: 1-56308-417-1]. (190 pages; $24.50)

Focusing on the new Science Education Standards, this activity-centered resource uses a wide variety of children's literature to integrate science across the elementary curriculum. With a thematic approach, it features the best in science trade books; stimulating "hands-on, minds-on" activities and experiments in life, physical, Earth, and space sciences; and a host of tips, ideas, and strategies that make teaching and learning science an adventure. A delightful array of creative suggestions, dynamic thematic units in all areas of science, and stimulating new science literature and activities highlight this resource.

Science Discoveries on the Net: An Integrated Approach [ISBN: 1-56308-823-1]. (315 pages; $27.50)

This book is designed to help teachers integrate the Internet into their science programs and enhance the scientific discoveries of students. The 88 units emphasize key concepts—based on national and state standards—throughout the science curriculum. Each unit is divided into five sections: Introduction (which includes basic background information on a topic), Research Questions (for students to investigate), Web Sites (the most current Internet sites on a topic), Children's Literature (the best books about a subject), and Activities (a host of "hands-on, minds-on" projects). The units are designed to energize any science curriculum and any classroom program.

Silly Salamanders and Other Slightly Stupid Stuff for Readers Theatre [ISBN: 1-56308-825-8]. (161 pages; $23.50)

The third entry in the "wild and wacky" readers theatre trilogy is just as crazy as the first two. How about these stories: "Snow White and the Seven Vertically Challenged Men," "The Big Bad Salamander and the Three Little Pigs," and "King Arthur and the Knights of the Polygon Table." This unbelievable resource offers students in grades 3–6 dozens of silly send-ups of well-known fairy tales, legends, and original stories guaranteed to fill any classroom with peels of laughter, howls of delight, and incredible language arts activities. It's a guaranteed winner!

Social Studies Discoveries on the Net: An Integrated Approach [ISBN: 1-56308-824-X]. (276 pages; $26.00)

This book is designed to help teachers integrate the Internet into their social studies programs and enhance the classroom discoveries of students. The 75 units emphasize key concepts—based on national and state standards—throughout the social studies curriculum. Each unit is divided into five sections: Introduction (which includes basic background information on a topic), Research Questions (for students to investigate), Web Sites (the most current Internet sites on a topic), Children's Literature (the best books about a subject), and Activities (a host of "hands-on, minds-on" projects). The units are designed to energize any social studies curriculum and any classroom program.

Social Studies Through Children's Literature: An Integrated Approach [ISBN: 0-87287-970-4]. (192 pages; $24.00)

Each of the 32 instructional units contained in this resource uses an activity-centered approach to elementary social studies, featuring children's picture books such as *Ox-Cart Man, In Coal Country,* and *Jambo Means Hello.* Each unit contains a book summary, social studies topic areas, curricular perspectives, critical thinking questions, and a large section of activities.

Tadpole Tales and Other Totally Terrific Titles for Readers Theatre [ISBN: 1-56308-547-X]. (115 pages; $18.50)

A follow-up volume to the best-selling *Frantic Frogs and Other Frankly Fractured Folktales for Readers Theatre*, this book provides primary-level readers (grades 1–4) with a humorous assortment of wacky tales based on well-known Mother Goose rhymes. For example, "Old MacDonald Had a Farm and, Boy, Did It Stink (E-I-E-I-O)." More than 30 scripts and dozens of classroom extensions will keep your students rolling in the aisles.

Index

About the Author

Tony is a nationally recognized children's literature expert well known for his energetic, fast-paced, and highly practical presentations for strengthening elementary science education. His dynamic and stimulating seminars have captivated thousands of teachers from coast to coast and border to border—all with rave reviews! His background includes extensive experience as a classroom teacher, curriculum coordinator, staff developer, author, professional storyteller, and university specialist in children's literature and science education.

Tony has written more than 50 teacher resource books in a variety of areas, including the hilarious *Tadpole Tales and Other Totally Terrific Treats for Readers Theatre* (Teacher Ideas Press), the award-winning *The Complete Phonemic Awareness Handbook* (Rigby), the best-selling *The Complete Guide to Thematic Units: Creating the Integrated Curriculum* (Christopher-Gordon), the celebrated *The Complete Science Fair Handbook*, co-authored with Isaac Asimov (Pearson Learning), and the extremely funny *Silly Salamanders and Other Slightly Stupid Stuff for Readers Theatre* (Teacher Ideas Press).

Not only is Tony an advocate for the integration of children's literature throughout the elementary curriculum, he is also the author of more than 20 highly acclaimed children's books including *Exploring the Rainforest* (Fulcrum), *Slugs* (Lerner), *Cannibal Animals* (Watts), *Under One Rock* (Dawn), *Exploring the Oceans* (Fulcrum), and *Zebras* (Lerner). He is currently a professor of education at York College in York, Pennsylvania. There, he teaches elementary methods courses in reading, language arts, science, and social studies. Additionally, he maintains a children's author Web site at http://www.afredericks.com, which is specifically designed for classrooms and schools across the country.

from *Teacher Ideas Press*

GLUES, BREWS, AND GOOS
Recipes and Formulas for Almost Any Classroom Project
Diana F. Marks

You've got to have it! This indispensable activity book pulls together hundreds of practical, easy recipes and formulas for classroom projects. From paints and salt map mixtures to volcanic action formulas, these kid-tested projects make learning authentic and enjoyable. All projects use ingredients that are easy to find and processes that are up-to-date. **Grades K–6.**
xvi, 179p. 8½x11 paper ISBN 1-56308-362-0

SCIENCE THROUGH CHILDREN'S LITERATURE, 2d Edition
Carol M. Butzow and John W. Butzow

The Butzows' groundbreaking, critically acclaimed, and best-selling resource has been thoroughly revised and updated with new titles and new activities for today's classroom. More than 30 exciting instructional units integrate all areas of the curriculum and serve as models to educators at all levels. Adopted as a supplementary text in schools of education nationwide, this resource features outstanding children's fiction books that are rich in scientific concepts yet equally well known for their strong story lines and universal appeal. **Grades K–3.**
xix, 205p. 8½x11 paper ISBN 1-56308-651-4

MULTICULTURAL FOLKTALES
Readers Theatre for Elementary Students
Suzanne I. Barchers

Introduce your students to other countries and cultures through these engaging readers theatre scripts based upon traditional folk and fairy tales. Representing more than 30 countries and regions, the 40 reproducible scripts are accompanied by presentation suggestions and recommendations for props and delivery. **Grades 1–5.**
xxi, 188p. 8½x11 paper ISBN 1-56308-760-X

SUPER SIMPLE STORYTELLING
A Can-Do Guide for Every Classroom, Every Day
Kendall Haven

Aside from guides to more than 40 powerful storytelling exercises, you'll find the Golden List of what an audience really needs from storytelling, a proven, step-by-step system for successfully learning and remembering a story, and the Great-Amazing-Never-Fail Safety Net to prevent storytelling disasters. This system has been successfully used by more than 15,000 educators across the country. **All Levels.**
xxvii, 229p. 8½x11 paper ISBN 1-56308-681-6

MORE SOCIAL STUDIES THROUGH CHILDREN'S LITERATURE
An Integrated Approach
Anthony D. Fredericks

These dynamic literature-based activities will help you energize the social studies curriculum and implement national and state standards. Each of these 33 units offers book summaries, social studies topic areas, critical thinking questions, and dozens of easy-to-do activities for every grade level. The author also gives practical guidelines for integrating literature across the curriculum, lists of Web sites useful in social studies classes, and annotated bibliographies of related resources. **Grades K–5.**
xix, 225p. 8½x11 paper ISBN 1-56308-761-8

For a free catalog or to place an order, please contact:
Teacher Ideas Press • Dept. B050 • P.O. Box 6633 • Englewood, CO • 80155-6633
800-237-6124 • www.lu.com/tip • Fax: 303-220-8843